The Power of Concentration

By Walter G. Oleksy

ARGUS COMMUNICATIONS
A Division of DLM, Inc.
Allen, Texas 75002

About the Author

Walter G. Oleksy is a Chicago-based freelance writer. He is the author of twenty-three books, a former feature writer for *The Chicago Tribune*, and an editor for three national magazines.

Material quoted from Melvin Powers, *A Practical Guide to Better Concentration* is reprinted by permission of Wilshire Book Co., North Hollywood, California.

Excerpt from *The Power of Concentration* by Bruno Furst, copyright 1972 by Lotte Furst & Gerrit Storm, copyright 1948, 1949 by Bruno Furst, is reprinted by permission of Doubleday & Co., Inc.

Cover Design by Joseph Essex
Photographs by Jaime Montemayor
Illustrations by Timothy M. Connelly

FIRST EDITION

©1981 Argus Communications
A Division of DLM, Inc.

Printed in the United States of America

Argus Communications
A Division of DLM, Inc.
One DLM Park
Allen, Texas 75002

International Standard Book Number: 0-89505-059-5

Dedicated to
Eric & Sandy Carlson

Contents

1

"What, Me Concentrate?"

Why should we want to concentrate better? Concentration can help us relax more, to sleep better, to accomplish more in our work or leisure, in learning or teaching, in coping with personal or family responsibilities, and in achieving greater rewards from prayer and/or meditation.

Before we begin dissecting the subject of concentration, some general thoughts are in order. Since you may be apprehensive that this study of concentration will be a little too deep or philosophical, perhaps a quote from the noted author Christopher Morley can dispel your fears on that count:

"No man is lonely while eating spaghetti—it requires so much attention."

A more scholarly observation on concentration comes from B. R. Haydon:

"The evidence of a superior genius is the power of intellectual concentration."

In the tone of this essay I hope to strike some middle ground between the attitudes expressed in the two quotations. I have attempted to include enough scientific evidence on concentration techniques to satisfy some readers, and enough practical guidance to satisfy others.

The dictionary defines *concentration* as "exclusive attention to one object; close mental application: He focused his concentration on the swinging pendulum." The key word in this definition is *attention,* which is defined by the *Encyclopedia Britannica* as "the selective process by which certain events in the environment come to be consciously perceived." In other words, while you are talking with a friend, you pay attention to the words he is speaking and ignore the voices of others around you. Or you attend to the picture on a television screen and fail to notice people who enter or leave the room. You listen attentively to the melody being played by a violinist at a concert and have only a vague awareness of the background provided by other instruments in the orchestra. A motorist may say after an accident, "I never saw the other car," even though the car was in his field of vision, because his attention was on the road ahead or his mind may have been on anything but his driving.

Do scientists know *how* we are able to concentrate? Unfortunately, they are only now at the beginning of their research into both the psychological and behavioral aspects of the question. Others, however, have sought answers to the questions of how we concentrate and how we can improve our ability to do so. These researchers may be specialists in education, rhetoric, learning, memory training, speaking, business, the arts, or sports. Interviews with many of them are reported in this book, together with summaries of their achievements in the study or development of concentration.

Techniques used by those practicing the Eastern

disciplines such as yoga will also be discussed here, among them focus, breathing, and relaxation exercises which enable us to achieve greater concentration. But what we come away with is a more Westernized approach, geared to our social and personal needs.

Finally, I have personally contacted many successful men and women in a variety of occupations who have been generous enough to share with us the techniques by which they have improved their own powers of concentration. Many top athletes will reveal their secrets of greater concentration in sports and leisure activities ranging from tennis and golf to jogging.

We are going to organize our thoughts in a progression, beginning with a look at studies on attention and listening. Later we will focus on ways parents and teachers can improve their own concentration and help children to concentrate better at home and at school. Everyone—students and instructors at high schools and colleges, workers in offices and in factories —can benefit from research conducted to help people concentrate better.

We will also talk about the roles of mood and environment in concentration—how to tune out noise and other distractions. We will learn methods of organizing thoughts and tasks that will help us to focus our attention better, as well as some helpful memory-training techniques. Finally, we will discuss physical and mental exercises that enable us to direct our energy and attention more efficiently.

Essentials of achieving better concentration include the following:

1. Interest

2. Organization of time
3. Organization of materials
4. Quiet
5. Focus
6. Environment
7. Mood
8. Attitude
9. Determination
10. Good health
11. Perseverence
12. Goal
13. Faith

Each of these elements will be analyzed in greater detail at some point in the book.

* * *

For most of us, the natural trend of our thoughts is to drift and spread. Our minds turn from one thing to another, dwelling on each just long enough for a pleasant and passing impression. This is the mind's natural gait and the one which we use for recreation. It is more like a stroll than a brisk walk or a mad dash to accomplish some task.

When we are tired of concentrated work, we turn on the television set, go to the movies, read a book, go for a jog, listen to music, or find other such mental escape. Our minds are still active, but without undue strain.

When we were children, we welcomed distraction. We were happy only when a lot was going on around us, and we jumped eagerly from one pleasure to the next. As we grew older, we found that it became harder to think and concentrate—at home, at school, or at work. We can blame most of the problem on the fact that often, we would rather be doing something else—talking, playing, shopping, attending to our garden or other hobbies—anything easier, more pleasant, less *Concentrated*.

To set up conditions in which we can concentrate better, we must avoid distractions such as noise, telephone calls, worry about deadlines or bills, and all conflicting interests. Our concentration will be better if we can find a place to be alone and shut out the rest of the world. But since that is seldom possible, we have to seek out alternatives which can at least partially achieve the same results. Many such alternatives will be found throughout this book.

It is said that not one person in a thousand is able to think upon one thing, to the exclusion of all else, for even sixty seconds. Imagine, then, how much time and energy we can save each day if we develop our powers of concentration. We will be able to get a great deal more done, better and more efficiently, and we will have more time left over which we can use for leisure activities. Many successful people maintain that the quality most needed for success in this life is *concentration*.

In its truest sense, concentration does not necessarily imply a blind, brainless straining after some end to the utter exclusion of all else. Whatever the task, whether it is playing golf or studying for an exam or preparing a sales campaign, to concentrate on it is to increase one's power of accomplishment.

Once you have decided that something is worth

doing, if you focus on that goal or purpose, if you throw yourself heart and soul into the doing of it, you will be surprised to see how much you *can* concentrate on it, and how quickly and well the task will be done. Where there is divided allegiance, where you allow your thoughts to wander from the work or play at hand, the task will neither get done nor be enjoyed.

One of the world's greatest photographers, Yousuf Karsh ("Karsh of Ottawa"), admits that he has no conscious techniques to help him achieve concentration, but ads:

"I do have total dedication to whomever I am photographing, and each subject is the most important focus in my life while I am photographing them."

By not allowing his allegiance to be divided, Karsh achieves total concentration on his task. The results have made him world-famous and rich.

At the heart of the three main ingredients of attention—observation, concentration, and memory—is *interest*, the basis of all three.

If the postman delivered a letter today informing you that you had just inherited a million dollars, you would have to read the information only briefly and never would forget any detail of it. Your interest would be so aroused, you would achieve total concentration.

You may argue that life is not full of letters announcing we have just become millionaires. How can we learn how to concentrate on the ordinary affairs of life? I will emphasize once again: with a certain amount of discipline and repetition, our ability to concentrate on a subject or task can be cultivated and strengthened.

Most of us can concentrate easily on a definite mechanical action, such as the moving of a piece of furniture, or upon some definite task—say, writing a letter or learning to memorize a short poem. The difficulty arises when we have to concentrate upon things which produce no immediate and definite result, such as the reading of a book, or of a complicated document like an insurance policy. We may think we have understood. We may believe that the task has been well done. There is nothing to show that we have not been concentrating and that we have imperfectly absorbed the contents—the evidence comes later.

On a larger scale, take the case of two executives. One is much more successful at focusing his attention than the other, and while this one succeeds in his work, the other fails. The failure doesn't perceive that he misses the mark because his attention is often scattered and his work habits disorganized. The successful man gets ahead because he has mastered the ability to concentrate—not only on the main project involved in his work, but on all its minute details.

Most of the truly successful people of the world, in politics, commerce, or professional work, subordinate everything to the main purposes of their lives. When they are at work they display extraordinary powers of concentration. These men and women often bewilder their fellow workers or achievers, because they never seem to work hard, or for any period of time. Their secret lies in their *power to concentrate,* and thus to obtain maximal results with a minimum of apparent effort.

"Concentration," said Ralph Waldo Emerson, "is the secret of success in politics, in war, in trade; in short in all the management of human affairs."

Concentration is a good habit that grows. A well-educated man is taught to concentrate when he is young. He is taught to assimilate interesting subjects. The less-educated learn to concentrate by trial and error. But for everyone, concentration in any particular direction eventually becomes automatic. Our unseen ally, the subconscious mind, begins to work for us.

For instance, after you first learned how to tie your own shoes as a child, you could do it without paying much attention to the task. You were concentrating subconsciously. The same applies to a lawyer cross-examining a witness. He doesn't have to say to himself, "Now, pay attention! Watch what you say or do, or you may make a terrible blunder." Subconsciously, he brings all his mental powers to bear on the moment. He makes his mind work as hard as it can in order to put across the point he wants to make.

The noted American philosopher and educator William James once said:

"The great end of all education is to make our nervous system our ally instead of our enemy. For this we must make automatic and habitual, as early as possible, as many useful actions as we can, and as carefully guard against the growing into ways that are likely to be disadvantageous."

Concentration, then, is an acquired habit of mind. Men are not born equal in their power to concentrate any more than they are born equal in their ability to play tennis or the stock market. But up to a point, everyone can improve his powers of concentration in every direction.

Remember, we are living in an age of specialization. Concentration is necessary not only to *do things*, but to *select* what to do. These days, no one can achieve great success unless he devotes all of his time and energy to some one thing. "Have the courage to be ignorant of a great number of things, in order to avoid the calamity of being ignorant of everything," said Sydney Smith, the English clergyman.

Speaking about application to study, the British essayist William Hazlitt said:

"It is wonderful how much is done in a short space, provided we set about it properly, and give our minds wholly to it. Let any one devote himself to any art or science ever so strenuously and he will still have leisure to make considerable progress in half a dozen other acquirements." This, he adds, explains the versatility of men like Leonardo da Vinci and Michaelangelo.

If you want to make your own work easier, take an interest in it. Focus your energies upon it. When interest is aroused, concentration follows.

Many people have been taught—even if perhaps unintentionally—*not* to concentrate. At home and at school, too many of us were not instilled with an intellectual curiosity which would make us want to learn as adults. If we developed an ambition for learning it probably grew despite many influences to the contrary.

Those who have been stimulated since childhood to be curious about things in their environment have little trouble in learning how to concentrate. If you do not yet have this type of curiosity, you would be wise to develop it, because it is basic to learning and concentration.

For now, the most important concept to grasp is that you *do* have the ability to improve your powers of concentration. If the author ever needed proof of that, it came in the writing of this essay, during which most of his major home appliances began malfunctioning or expiring at the same time—his automobile, washing machine, tape recorder for receiving phone interviews, and even the much too expensive electric typewriter on which this manuscript was written.

All this occurred with the first signs of spring, the start of the noisy season in which all bedlam breaks forth outdoors after a long but relatively tranquil winter. Neighborhood dogs began barking, cats began crying, city sewer workers began jackhammering in the streets, and balmy afternoons brought gleefully screaming boys and girls into the tot park across the street.

"What, *me* concentrate?" you ask. Of course you can! All it really takes is the *wanting*, over all obstacles. And maybe a deadline helps a little.

2

The Essentials of Attentiveness

The scientific community still knows very little for certain about the biological or physiological means by which we focus our attention on certain things to the exclusion of others. If one word were to sum up what most researchers *think* is the prime factor in concentration, it would be *interest*. If we are truly interested in anything, we will have little trouble concentrating on it, whether it is solving math problems or painting landscapes or playing handball.

"We are at the very beginning of studying how the mind is able to concentrate," says Dr. Helen Neville of the Salk Institute in California, who is conducting research into selective attention. "This is because it is just now possible to monitor brain functions in man, utilizing newly introduced electro-physiological techniques, the way we have been able to monitor them in animals."

Other researchers at Salk Institute are investigating the strong possibility that "tendrils" connecting the base of the brain with all parts of its structure may be the body's "concentration center." Apparently these tendrils take input from our senses—sight, hearing, smell, taste—and, if this input is deemed important, send an impulse to the brain. Think of the way a mother may be alerted, though she is sound asleep, when her infant cries in another room. A signal to her brain warns her, "Hey, your child needs you!"

Salk researchers also are experimenting with the drug naloxone, an opiate antagonist which they believe may be used to improve selective attention in normal people. The drug may be able to reduce some of liquor's effects on alcoholics as well.

It has long been known in the scientific community that our sensory capacities, interests, needs, past experiences, and level of alertness or wakefulness are all factors which may be important in determining the direction of attention at any given time.

Experiments have attempted to answer such questions as: How long can attention be maintained on one particular stimulus object? What conditions influence fluctuation or shifting of attention? Can two or more objects be attended to at one time?

Simple answers cannot be given to these questions because numerous conditions affect the experimental results obtained. Fluctuations of attention (or concentration) may be due to adaptation of the sense organs, to slight movements of the sense organs (particularly in the case of vision), or to slight changes in the stimulus conditions.

Studies of electroencephalograms, records of the electrical activity of the brain produced by means of electrodes placed on the skull or directly on the brain, reveal that a change in the pattern of recorded activity occurs if a light or sound is presented to a resting, relaxed subject. The brain wave pattern changes from one of slow waves of high amplitude to one of fast

14

waves of relatively low amplitude. This change is referred to as activation of the EEG, or arousal response. It seems to be related closely to the degree of general alertness or attentiveness of the subject whose electroencephalogram is being recorded.

Experiments on animals show that a similar arousal response may be produced by electrical stimulation of the brain stem reticular formation. This structure consists of a complex of nuclei extending along the core of the brain stem from the level of the medulla to the thalamus. Evidence suggests that the brain stem reticular formation plays an important role in the maintenance and control of attention, alertness, and consciousness, all of which bear importantly on our ability to concentrate.

Research into the functions of the right and left hemispheres of the brain also is expected to help result in a better understanding of how we concentrate. "Superlearning," a concept pioneered by Sheila Ostrander and Lynn Schroeder, suggests that if the left half of the brain (which controls logical, rational, analytical thinking) and the right half of the brain (which is responsible for intuition, creativity, and imagination) were to perform in harmony with the body, a person could be capable of increased performance.

Superlearning is reportedly possible when a relaxed state is achieved by means of synchronized rhythm. If the body is relaxed and the heartbeat is lowered from about seventy-five beats a minute to about sixty beats a minute, it should then be possible to accomplish even very difficult mental tasks effortlessly and without stress.

Such a relaxed state can be induced, according to Superlearning, and the mind kept alert and focused, if we listen to music with a very specific rhythm. The music should provide a "sonic message" that eliminates the stress of intensive mental work.

Thus far, studies have centered around slow movements of 60 beats a minute in 4/4 time from Baroque concerti of the masters such as Bach. Rhythmic breathing also is considered very important in achieving high levels of concentration for Superlearning.

More discussion on music as an aid to concentration will be found in chapter 7 on mood and environment, while breathing exercises are described in chapter 11.

Recent scientific research shows that the two hemispheres of the brain mediate and process different kinds of information and handle different kinds of tasks and problems.

The left hemisphere, the more dominant and "overdeveloped" side of the brain in most Americans, specializes in verbal and numerical information processed in a linear fashion. It is the active, verbal, logical, rational, and analytic part of our brain, drawing conclusions based on a logical order of things. It figures things out sequentially, step by step, part by part, one element after another in an ordered way, proceeding in terms of linked thoughts, one idea directly following another to a convergent conclusion. The left brain utilizes precise, exact connotations such as right/wrong, yes/no, etc.

The right hemisphere is the intuitive, experimental, nonverbal part of our brain and deals in images and in

16

holistic, relational grasping of complex configurations and structures. It creates metaphors, analogies, and new combinations of ideas, making leaps of insight based on hunches, feelings, incomplete data, patterns, and imagery. It perceives through pattern recognition and spatial references where things are in relation to other things and how parts connect to form wholes.

To better grasp the differences and compare the functions and modes of the left and right hemispheres of the brain, study the following comparison.

Left Hemisphere	Right Hemisphere
Verbal—language, speech, counting, naming, reading	Nonverbal—use of imagery
Explicit—definite, clearly stated	Tacit—unspoken, silent
Controlled, consistent	Emotive, affect-laden
Realistic thinking—strong orientation to reality	Fantasy—reverie, day-dreaming
Dominant	Nondominant or quiet
Intellectual, formal	Sensuous, experimental
Sharp focal awareness	Diffuse awareness
Active	Receptive
Linear time—keeps track of time, placing one thing after another in sequence	Timelessness, non-temporality—without sense of time
Mathematical, scientific	Artistic, musical, symbolic
Objective	Subjective
Judgmental, evaluative	Nonjudgmental, noncritical

Convergent thinking—one conclusion or alternative, one meaning	Divergent thinking—many conclusions or alternatives; many meanings
Rational—bases conclusions on facts and reason	Nonrational—doesn't require basis of reason or facts
Conscious processing	Subconscious or preconscious processing
Literal meaning	Metaphorical/analogical meaning

Because one hemisphere of our brain is dominant over the other, generally speaking we can concentrate better on the subjects or objects which our dominant hemisphere programs us to be "more tuned into." Knowing our personal strengths and weaknesses, we ought to be able to identify which hemisphere is dominant in our brain. We should then try to develop the recessive hemisphere, working harder to tap its resources. At the very least, knowing the strengths and weaknesses we have from the dominant and recessive hemipheres of our brain can help explain why we attend closely to some things and not to others.

No matter which side of our brain dominates our thinking, paying attention and concentrating is often an exhausting mental and physical process for people who are unaccustomed to it. The essence of concentration is a centering of the full powers of the mind on the task in hand. A tired body and mind can't accomplish this to the best advantage, and many psychological and environmental factors also must be controlled in order to increase our attentive capabilities.

Attention is a habit of mind. You can force yourself to pay attention, but if you want to be consistent and effective in concentration, you will benefit from practicing the guidelines and techniques offered in the following pages by researchers and achievers in many varied fields.

"The power of sustained attention is an amazing gift," the educator Douglas V. Steere has said. "Philosophers, quite rightly, seized upon it as a compelling piece of evidence for man's being free and not determined. We can listen or we can relax our attention or direct it elsewhere.

"This power we possess of turning on or withholding the spotlight of attention from that which confronts us is a gift so close to the core of what makes us persons that other powers fade before it; and in each exercise of it there is something self-confirming about our status as free and responsible persons.

"When we see this gift of concentrated attention operating superbly in others, we are overcome with a longing to possess more of it ourselves.

"The New Testament records instance after instance of this power of attention achieved in great measure by Jesus. The miserable taxgatherer Zaccheus, who was looked upon as a local quisling grown wealthy at the expense of others and beneath their contempt, sat perched on the limb of the tree when Jesus passed. Jesus seemed to see in this man something no townsman saw, a new man waiting to be born, and the account says that He called out to him to come down and be His host for the day. This power of attention seems to give to those who possess it new eyes for invisibles."

Steere tells of his visit with Albert Schweitzer at the doctor's jungle hospital in Africa some years ago:

"I saw this man at all hours of the day and night carrying on his work. Whether he was organizing a crew of reluctant Africans to unload a boat of lumber, or guiding the laying of a cement foundation and floor for a fruit cellar, or practicing on his steel piano, or working on his book deep into the night, or on his knees utterly absorbed in watching a ten-minute-old antelope try to rally its long pipe stem legs to make its first erect stand in this world, Doctor Schweitzer seemed to be giving to each task his entire, complete, and undivided attention. He seemed to live for nothing except that moment, and to be utterly and completely open to the needs of that moment, and to receive the full impact of the impressions of that moment.

"Many of us want the power of sustained attention, but we do not want what brings it about. *The Imitation of Christ* (Thomas àKempis, 1380-1471) says 'All desire peace, but they do not desire the things that lead to true peace,' or again, 'All desire to contemplate, but they do not desire what leads to true contemplation.' The deep hunger and positive motivation required to produce attention depend upon what we really want most.

"Dogged as men are today by the threat of cosmic arson, there is a sense in which our world in both East and West seems to be moving in a profound somnambulism, climbing along window ledges and crossing parapets that are so dangerous that we dare not awaken lest we stagger and pitch headlong into the abyss. It is in such a time that we need men and women with so great a power of sustained attention that each might take as his point of intent to seek 'to walk through the dream of life as one awake.'"

Another viewpoint on the powers of attention is expressed by Frederick B. Robinson, former president of the College of the City of New York, writing on *How to Make Your Mind Behave*:

"The first point which should be emphasized about concentration is this: The men who achieve important positions in life depend less upon their natural special aptitudes or inherited gifts, than on this *acquired ability* to fix the attention upon any specific problem and to hold the mind to that problem until they have seen it through. Any man or woman who gets anywhere has to learn to make his mind behave in the directions which it ought to take in order that he or she can persist in affairs that are vital . . . no matter what drudgery is involved.

"As for the mental processes involved in the act of concentration, the psychologists still are in the dark. Indeed, we are no nearer a solution of the mystery of the mind, in its ultimate direction and control, than we are, in the final analysis, to the mystery of electricity.

"Nevertheless, though we cannot satisfactorily explain what the mind really is, we *can* employ certain methods to help us control, develop, and apply our mental powers, just as we employ certain methods to generate, control, and use electricity, though we do not know what *this* force really *is*."

Robinson says that not as a psychologist but as a practical man he has found four simple principles of

21

great use to him in developing and applying such mental powers as he has to the varied tasks and problems he has to face. They are as follows:

1. Cultivate a keen and active interest — a zest — in the subject to be mastered or the task to be performed, which is of primary importance if the mind is to work efficiently.

2. Learn to amass in an orderly way the raw materials necessary for your thinking. Get the facts! Stress, in due proportion, those which bear directly on the problem under consideration. Subordinate, or sift out, those which are of minor importance, or irrelevant.

3. If you want to think hard and hit hard, you must learn to take it easy. The most *efficient* use of our mental and physical energy is likewise the most economical.

4. There is evidently something in the mind which, after a sustained effort, becomes temporarily exhausted but recovers and goes on trying and trying, so that the solution of the problem may come in an altogether unexpected way. That is to say, at times our mental processes continue at work subconsciously. To a certain extent, we can *make the subconscious work for us.*

Clifton Fadiman, whose genius was putting his finger on the pulse of our times and reminding us of the stumbling blocks in the way of achievement, deplored the growing decline of attention not only in America but everywhere he traveled.

Fadiman warned, "We must beware" of assuming that the prime causes of the decline of attention "are to be found in such symptoms as the digest, advertising, the radio, television, the gossip column, picture magazine, the soap opera, the mass-newspaper, the comic book, the movies, the monosyllabic novel. They aid in the relaxation of attention, but they do not cause it. They are merely carriers of the germ."

Fadiman said that for the fundamental causes of the decline of attention, we must go back to a quotation from William Wordsworth, the English poet, in the preface to the 1802 edition of his *Lyrical Ballads*:

"A multitude of causes, unknown to former times, are now acting with a combined force to blunt the discriminating powers of the mind, and, unfitting it for all voluntary exertion, to reduce it to a state of almost savage torpor. The most effective of these causes are the great national events [revolutions and wars] which are daily taking place, and the increasing accumulation of men in cities, where the uniformity of their occupations produces a craving for extraordinary incident, which the rapid communication of intelligence hourly gratifies."

Fadiman said that it is interesting to note that the decline of attention had been clearly spotted as far back as 1802, and also that some of its causes — nationalism and industrialism — were philosophically identified. Concluded Fadiman:

"The fundamental causes of the decline of attention lie deep in the history of the last three hundred years and are almost surely connected with the rise of aggressive nationalism and the victory of the industrial revolution. At some point in the not very remote past, a profound shift in our thinking took place. An interest in altering and vanquishing the environment by means of mechanical techniques plus an interest in

23

material accumulation began to oust our traditional interest in discovering the nature of man and expounding his relation to God.

"Nationalism set itself up against universal thought, substituting for it local and temporal dogma. Industrialism erected definite, easily understandable standards of values, quite at variance with the ethical, religious, and esthetic standards that had, at least in theory, prevailed before its time. These standards 'paid off' — that is, the man who lived by them found himself becoming 'successful' or 'adjusted.'

"It seemed more useful to fix the attention on a new system of double-entry bookkeeping or the mechanism of the internal-combustion engine than on *Hamlet*. It *was* more useful; it was also more enjoyable.

"Most of us want to be part of contemporary history, and if contemporary history does not demand of us any rigorous ordering of the faculty of attention, we will either allow it to decline or we will fix it upon those objects or processes in which the majority of our fellow-citizens seem to be genuinely interested.

"The humanist will cry out against all this; but he forgets that humanism itself is no more than three thousand years old, a short parenthesis in history. At one time, the mental habits of the caveman prevailed over the earth. There seems no absolute reason why the mental habits of George Orwell's robot man of 1984 should not come to prevail during the next few hundred years. Those reactionaries who believe that man is unchangeably a rational soul will have faith that Orwell's world, too, will pass; and that man is bound to return to the pursuit of those goods Socrates and Jesus pointed out to him.

"But it is doubtful that this return will on a large scale come to pass in our time. For the moment, the humanist would seem constrained to bide his time and conserve the faculty of attention as the church conserved the riches of the classical tradition during what is unfairly called the Dark Ages."

In the quarter-century since Fadiman expressed those thoughts on the decline of attention, it is apparent that the decline has slipped even farther. But there finally does seem to be a faint light at the end of the tunnel, as more people are today coming to realize they may have been missing something by allowing the distractions and values of the modern world to rob them of their powers of concentration.

That more of us are becoming eager for improved attention and greater concentration is evident from the openness with which we now receive information of new scientific and medical discoveries from television news, magazines, and the front pages of our newspapers. Interest in science and health is perhaps greater today than ever before in our history, as we pay more attention to new advances which can help us to live healthier, happier, longer, more productive and enriched lives.

Reflecting this interest, if not actual craving, on the part of the public, television and motion pictures are now delving into subjects involving mind expansion. A large segment of the public is tuning in to movies such as "Altered States," which point us inward toward adventures of the mind rather than outward to a focus on mere special effects.

Since man has already made such phenomenal advances in expanding his horizons into outer space —walking on the moon, viewing satellite pictures transmitted to Earth from Saturn and beyond — the mind is becoming the last frontier of exploration. Perhaps it will be our greatest adventure.

3

How to Listen Better

It is generally agreed that we have greater difficulty concentrating while listening than we have during any other stage of communication.

Some researchers believe that this is because when we listen, we must achieve a type and degree of concentration that is peculiar to aural communication. The difference apparently stems from the fact that we think much more quickly than we talk.

Most of us speak at a rate of about 125 words a minute. While this may sound fast, it is actually quite slow for the human brain, whose more than 13 billion cells operate more rapidly and in more complicated patterns than the "brains" of even the latest-model computers.

While many who study the brain disagree as to how the brain functions when we think, most psychologists agree that the basic medium of thought is language. But while we may be able to speak only 125 words per minute, words do race through our heads much more swiftly than that.

Many people can read and comprehend 1,200 words per minute. Some who have undergone speed-reading instruction are able to read even more rapidly while still retaining a great deal of what they read. One speed-reader was able to scan for facts at the rate of about 10,000 words per minute, later scoring over 80 percent on a test of what he had read.

Most of us can comfortably comprehend a speaker who talks to us at a rate much faster than 125 words per minute. Many can grasp speech at more than 300 words per minute without losing comprehension significantly. We could probably understand even more words spoken per minute were it not for an inability on the part of the speaker to pronounce his words more distinctly when speaking very rapidly.

So, while our brain can receive and comprehend words programmed into it at very rapid speeds, when we listen to spoken words we ask our brain to slow down in dealing with them. Perhaps we should deal with the problem by slowing down our thinking, to adjust for the 125 words per minute we are receiving. But we tend not to do this. Instead, when we listen we keep thinking at high speed while receiving words spoken at a much slower speed. This allows us to be able to do something else with our brain in addition to receiving the 125 words per minute. Besides listening, we are thinking.

Therein lies a basic problem in attending to what we hear. Since we are both hearing and thinking while listening, we often lose concentration on what is being said. Our thinking generally sets our minds wandering, picking up distractions around us as we listen, or sending our thoughts off on tangents far outside the listening environment. That is why we may be lulled into a hazy blur when a slow and perhaps dull speaker is only able to claim our attention for a short time.

Soon we find our minds wandering to that sunny afternoon on the beach last summer.

We may be on our concentration toes while listening to a fast-talking used car salesman trying to sell us a lemon, but if a slow and soft-spoken encyclopedia salesman gets our ear, we may soon be mesmerized into oblivion, and happily. While the used car salesman may have our total concentration, the encyclopedia salesman's dulcet tones more slowly spoken may put us to sleep.

When our minds have spare time to think while we are listening, whatever the reason, we are losing our concentration. The trick is to be able to use this spare listening time efficiently to help us better concentrate on what we are hearing. These are some of the basic concepts on good listening presented by Ralph G. Nichols, a professor emeritus of the University of Minnesota's Department of Rhetoric who is often called "the father of listening" because of his lifelong study of the subject.

Dr. Nichols reports that students tested in the art of listening were able to listen well when they made good use of their spare time while listening. They had the following four habits in common:

1. The listener was able to think ahead of the speaker. He would try to guess what the speaker was leading up to and tried to focus his attention on what conclusions could be drawn from what the speaker was then saying.

2. The listener weighed the verbal evidence being presented to determine whether the speaker's points could be supported by his words.

31

3. Every so often during the speech, the listener would mentally review what the speaker had said so far.

4. While listening to the speaker, the listener "listened between the lines," searching for meanings that the speaker may not have put into words.

Dr. Nichols maintains that the speed at which we think, compared to that at which we hear words spoken, allows us plenty of time to accomplish all four of these mental tasks while we listen.

"I have always been concerned with what is called 'intellectual curiosity,'" says Dr. Nichols. "I think it is the key to concentration and also the key to effective listening, because to be a good listener you have to concentrate on what the speaker is saying. You have to analyze whether he has a pattern of organization, detect that pattern, and so on.

"The business of maintaining curiosity among young people and through into adult years is a tremendous task. The newborn child is a bundle of curiosity. He's interested in smell, taste, changes of temperature, and then he gets interested in sounds. Eventually he gets interested in expressing himself, etc.

"Unfortunately, I feel, in many homes and indeed in some schools, this intellectual curiosity is methodically destroyed. How is it destroyed? Usually by reprimand, reproval, punishment — penalty of some kind. But if this curiosity were nourished, I don't believe there is any end to what man could accomplish, because people like Benjamin Franklin, Thomas Edison, and Albert Einstein, who have really changed the destiny of man, were all intellectually curious

32

people.

"If we could go to a Sears and Roebuck store and *buy* intellectual curiosity by the ounce or pound, we'd have lines from New York to San Francisco. Everyone would want to get their ration of this thing.

"The difference between creativity and productivity and nothing accomplished at all is intellectual curiosity. But if this intellectual curiosity is so tremendous, it seems to me that any educator, any businessman, any intellectual ought to desperately be trying to nourish it, instead of letting it get systematically ruined.

"If we can improve the curiosity a child is born with and not drive it out of him, by reprimand or whatever method we use, and replace *approval* to build curiosity, we are giving that child one of the greatest tools toward success and happiness we can give him.

"The 'approval factor' is not only of tremendous importance in becoming a good listener, it also is a significant factor in curiosity. The two are almost identical.

"I believe that listening is the most economical way to learn, if we listen correctly.

"Mental efficiency is the foundation for all efficiency. It is the human brain that has turned a savage into a king, a lowly wage earner into a captain of industry. We cannot even perceive the heights to which our brains may yet carry us. To climb those heights we shall need to preserve and nourish the curiosity we still possess. If we succeed in this, concentration upon each task arising can be achieved. No surer prescription for success can be written."

Centuries before man learned to communicate by

means of written symbols, he communicated with others by word of mouth. The earliest educators such as Aristotle and Plato taught their pupils primarily through lectures. Even most of the literature of ancient nations or peoples was kept alive by oral tradition. Ages ago, listening was an indispensable art and the ear held precedence over the eye. One educator, Bonaro W. Overstreet, expressed this well:

"The individual who, in the long preliterate stages of history, had no keen ability as a listener, must have remained a prisoner within his own small cell of experience."

But with the invention of the printing press five centuries ago, listening slowly gave way to reading. Man in the Western world became increasingly print-minded and the emphasis in education switched from use of the ear to use of the eye. The art of reading became the dominant faculty for gaining an education.

In recent years, first radio and then television have tended to bring the ear back into a prominent place in receiving information. Today, the spoken word, largely from television and radio, has taken the lead from the written word to become the most powerful medium of communication the world has ever known.

Shortly after World War II, Wendell Johnson, another educator, voiced concern that the tremendous increase in the amount of spoken words from the mass media would serve us well only if we learned to improve our listening habits:

"As the world grows more ominously voluble by the hour, the words we hurl at each other are no more confusing and maddening, or clarifying and calming, than our habits of listening permit them to be. Until they reach our ears they are mere sound waves, gentle breezes, harmless as a baby's breath. It is through the alchemy of listening that they become transformed into the paralyzing and convulsant toxins of distrust and hate — or the beneficial potions of good will and intelligence."

What troubles others concerned about problems involved in listening is that our eyes have been trained to receive visual information, but our ears have not. Most instruction which school children get in listening is limited to almost useless admonitions like "Pay attention!" and "Listen carefully!" Listening, at all education levels, has been a neglected language art for generations.

One reason the art of listening has been neglected in teaching is that children begin to acquire listening skills at a very early age. Before they start school at five or six years of age, they have learned how to listen and how to speak quite well. Without any formal education, they appear to have learned already how to listen and how to speak. They seem to be in amazing control of oral language.

Instructors therefore suppose that it is not necessary to instruct children in listening or even in speaking. Instead they focus on teaching reading and writing, at the virtual exclusion of listening. Children are frequently tested in reading ability, seldom if ever in listening ability. Since the early 1950s, some effort has been made to focus more attention on listening as a vital language art at all educational levels.

Researchers believe that reading and listening have

much in common. Training in one seems to support the other, but competence in one does not necessarily mean competence in the other. Some good readers are poor listeners and some good listeners are poor readers. Listening, it is believed, is the most important of the language arts.

Some progress has been made in developing teaching skills regarding listening. Four basic steps are suggested:

1. A favorable listening climate must be established. Good listening habits are not instilled in students by making them participate in question-answer sessions, by rehashing textbook assignments, or by assigning book reports, which merely tend to prove whether or not a student has read the book. If students are to speak effectively, they must be encouraged to have something worthwhile to say, someone to whom they can say it, and an ability to say it. The same holds true for listening. Students should have something worthwhile to listen to, a reason for listening, someone to whom they care to listen, and a faculty for listening.

2. Pupils at all grade levels should be told why good listening habits are important and what skills they must learn to be good listeners.

3. There must be an awareness, on the part of both students and teachers, of the similarities and differences in the receiving language arts — reading and listening. For example, in reading the reader sets the pace of communication for himself, while in listening the speaker sets the pace for the listener.

4. Probably the most important factor in a program of good listening is a provision for systematic instruc-

tion in the art of listening. Subjects could include narration, exposition, persuasion, lyric poetry, dramatic productions, informal conversation, group discussion, and both structured and unstructured speech.

Listening with a high degree of concentration is a problem most people share, whether they are students, parents, workers or whatever. A recent survey revealed that most white-collar workers spend at least forty percent of their workday listening, yet most of them have only twenty-five percent efficiency in concentrating on what they hear.

Grade school teachers spend over half their class time talking to students, and the percentage is even greater in high school and college. College students spend over eighty percent of their class time listening to lectures, since this is considered to be the most effective and cheapest way to spread knowledge among the most learners at one time. But research reveals that college students who hear a ten-minute lecture can recall only half of it immediately afterward, and two weeks later retain no more than one-fourth of the message.

What researchers into listening tend to agree upon is that learning through listening is mainly an inside job — inside action on the part of the listener.

Many major corporations, recognizing the importance of developing effective listening in their executives, have added courses in the art of listening to their training programs. Pioneers in the effort include The Sperry Corporation, American Telephone and Telegraph, General Motors, Ford, Dow Chemical, and Western Electric. Sperry is said to have turned the art of listening into a "corporate crusade," offering a free pamphlet to the public with cartoon characters and suggestions on effective listening, including admonitions like "Concentrate!" and "Don't jump to conclusions while listening."

Sperry's approach to listening defines three major barriers to good listening: physical conditions such as fatigue or hunger, distractions such as outside noise and interruptions, and hearing problems.

Dr. Ralph Nichols and his colleagues at the University of Minnesota have formulated ten basic guidelines which can be applied by anyone to improve his or her mastery of the art of good listening. They generously share these tips with us here:

1. *Be interested.* It is essential that you be interested in the topic under discussion. If you are not interested, your concentration will fall off drastically after just the first few sentences. If you fail to force yourself to generate interest in the topic, you will tend to rationalize your inattention with the excuse that the subject or speaker is dry and boring. Since you may not be able to get up and leave, make a determined effort to become more interested in what the speaker is saying.

Perhaps the best way to become more interested is to ask yourself what you can *use* out of what is being said. Is the speaker saying anything you can turn into ideas, money, or something to make you happier?

G.K. Chesterton once said, "There is no such thing as an uninteresting subject; there are only uninteresting people."

2. *Don't hate the speaker.* If you ignore a speaker's poor delivery, constant referral to notes, or other dis-

tractions, you can focus instead on what you can get out of what he is saying. Don't hate the speaker for his loud tie, unpressed trousers, nasal twang, or monotonous voice. If you are tolerant of his shortcomings as a speaker, your ability to concentrate on what you hear will rise considerably. Likewise, do not fall in love with his melodic voice or charisma. *Listen* to what he is saying; do not concentrate on his style.

3. *Do not jump the gun.* Do not be too eager to have your own viewpoint known. As bad as losing interest in a speaker is becoming too quick to think you know his position and deciding you are totally opposed to it. If you make up your mind too fast that you have an opposing viewpoint, you will tend to concentrate more on your rebuttal than upon the speaker's argument.

It is only human nature in this situation to focus your attention on how the speaker is stomping on the grapes of your own pet ideas or viewpoint. You begin forming questions or arguments mentally, to shoot down the speaker's position. But while you are concentrating on your rebuttal, you probably will not be listening to what the speaker is saying next, which may even cover your intended rebuttal.

Give the speaker time to tell everything he has to say before attempting to argue with him. It is always important to withhold evaluation until your comprehension is complete.

4. *Listen for ideas.* Get into the habit of listening for ideas rather than for facts. A speaker may string a lot of facts together to support his argument, and while you are concentrating on remembering first one, then two, then half a dozen facts, you may be missing the

point he is trying to make. You may be able to memorize the facts but you will not be attending to his intended message. This problem is a major reason why only about twenty-five percent of persons listening to formal instruction are able to understand the speaker's main idea.

To overcome this listening problem it is important to develop the ability to recognize patterns by which speakers organize their material. These include transitional language, use of recapitulation, and other techniques of formal speaking.

5. *Be a smart note-taker*. Taking notes during a talk can be helpful in focusing your attention on the material, but often speakers are not carefully organized. If your notes follow a disorganized speaker's trend of thought, you will wind up with notes just as disorganized.

Other problems in note-taking during a lecture include taking down either too many notes or too few. Instead of writing copious notes in shorthand or in our own abbreviated longhand, or jotting down just a few key words or concepts from a speaker, it is wisest to take brief but meaningful notes which can act as springboards for your memory later on.

6. *Put some effort into your listening*. Listening often is not easy. We may wish we could relax while the focus is not on us and let the speaker do all the work. We prefer to unwind from physical or intellectual effort, pretending we are alert to the speaker, while actually we daydream.

Slouching in a chair may be comfortable, but it keeps us from paying proper attention to what we hear. Greater concentration can be achieved in listening if we sit correctly and establish eye contact with the speaker.

7. *Tune out distractions.* Often, speakers either have to fight visual and aural distractions or create some of their own — all of which can distract us, the listener. Poor listeners will magnify those distractions, while good listeners will try hard to eliminate them or at least to tune them out.

8. *Become a more experienced listener.* Most people tend not to challenge themselves in what they listen to, exposing their minds primarily to light, recreational input. When they are met with the challenge of listening to heavier, more thought-provoking or concentration-demanding information, they cannot cope with it. Confusion or boredom sets in, and their attention drifts. Good listeners work at challenging themselves more, so they can accept more technical or complex material.

9. *Beware of prejudices.* A good listener does not allow himself to get emotionally upset or deafened when a speaker treads on his prejudices. Often, words can trigger our anger, frustration, or prejudices. Words such as *communist, dope addict, gay, hippie,* or even *mother-in-law* can trigger such emotion in us that we tune out what the speaker is trying to tell us. A good listener learns not to let words become like red flags waved in front of a bull.

10. *Control leftover thinking time.* If our minds tend to wander when a speaker talks slower than our mind can comprehend, we must try to make the most of our excess thinking time while listening. As noted earlier

in this chapter, the good listener does not allow his mind to wander during this extra listening time. Instead he uses it to pay closer attention to what is being said, looking for greater value in the thoughts of the speaker.

"Not capitalizing on thought speed is the greatest single handicap in listening well," says Dr. Nichols. "Yet, through listening training, this same problem can be converted into our greatest asset."

Dr. Nichols's successor at the University of Minnesota, Dr. Lyman K. Steil, has additional thoughts on listening better:

"One of the things we continue to find is, when we ask people in our testing to identify the major problems they face as listeners, the things they list continue to be lack of concentration, mental tangencies their thinking goes off on, and daydreaming.

"One thing we work very hard at to improve listening is to suggest ways of focusing, sharpening, and enhancing the ability to concentrate.

"Many students say they can only pay attention to a speaker if he says something they are interested in hearing. But then we ask them very candidly 'At what point do you determine you're interested in something?' With listening, the basic problem is that you will never know you're interested in something until *after* you've listened to it.

"There is a concept I've developed called the 'Value Moment of Listening' which basically means that we'll never know the value of what we're listening to until after we've heard it and understood it. As a consequence, you listen better if you are constantly looking for items that will be of potential immediate or delayed long-term value to you. That way your concentration is kept in focus and heightened."

4

Concentration and the Learning Process

Most problems with children, whether they are normal or hyperactive, involve getting them to calm down and be quiet and/or more productive in their play or study. Why do many children find it difficult to concentrate on their studies? And how can parents and teachers help them to become better achievers through improved concentration?

Educators believe that some children do better than others in school because their parents have read to them since infancy and have set a tone at home for the value of education.

Taking this concept a step further is Dr. Benjamin S. Bloom, a professor of education at the University of Chicago. In his recent book, *All Our Children Learning,* Bloom suggest that if children are to develop their intellectual capacities to the fullest, parents must work actively with the schools to support learning.

Some educators believe that socioeconomic status of the family is a key ingredient in a child's school success. Bloom, however, emphasizes that it is what parents do in the home, not their status, that is a powerful determinant in school achievement.

Bloom suggests several ways by which parents can help their children concentrate better so they can succeed in school. Some degree of structure and routine in the home is essential for good work habits in school, he maintains. Children from homes with clear structure—shared responsibilities and set routines—learn better in school, he finds, than children from homes where each member of the family does his own thing whenever he wants to do it.

Clear plans are necessary for work and play, and for the sharing of duties and household chores among family members. A clear allocation of time should be provided—to eat, sleep, play, work, study, and read. Precautions should be taken so that television-watching and play do not take precedence over other activities.

"School learning is a long and difficult process for most children," Bloom says. "Unless there is a great deal of support and encouragement, children will find it difficult to maintain their interest in and commitment to the learning."

Since most children encounter problems in some aspect of learning, they may need help to overcome these obstacles. One way parents can help in this is to praise their children for good schoolwork. They also can speak approvingly to others about what their children have accomplished.

Bloom believes that parents must monitor their children's schoolwork, so they are aware of what the children are learning in school and of their special strengths and weaknesses. Parents must be willing to give their children help in studying, when needed. They must constantly encourage their children to do their best.

Parents may recognize that children need a quiet

place to study. But they should emphasize that wherever this quiet place is, it should be used regularly.

Since much learning takes place outside of the classroom and the home, often in informal activities, parents and children should share interests in hobbies, games, trips to museums, concerts, and other cultural activities which have educational value.

Television viewing in the home should be controlled. If the tube is going day and night, used as a free babysitter by weary parents, no time is being set aside for learning experiences such as reading.

Friends of mine in Ohio told me half a dozen years ago that when their television set broke down, they held a family conference about whether or not to have it repaired. Father, mother, and two preteen-aged children agreed to try living without the TV set for a while, as an experiment. The set went into a hall closet unrepaired and has remained there.

"We do more together now," says the father. "We talk to each other more, we play games such as cards and Monopoly and Scrabble together. We go bike riding together, take more picnics, spend more evenings reading books and listening to good music. We're having a wonderful time, getting to know each other better, since we turned off the TV set. And the kids are doing much better in school. They concentrate better on their work and they learn better. But the funny thing is, none of us feels we're deprived. We just learned that we didn't need television to enjoy ourselves."

Ideally, Bloom suggests, a family should discuss the ideas, views, and subjects they come upon in their reading. Daily events, news, and selected television programs can stimulate families in discussions which can benefit each member.

"What is most essential is that each member of the family have an opportunity to express and share his or her ideas and views with others," Bloom emphasizes. "The discussions should take place frequently and in an informal way."

Parents should continually emphasize high academic aspirations from their children.

"It is usually the parents who set the standards for the child's learning in and out of school," says Bloom. "This includes the quality of the work the child is expected to do as well as the grades or marks he or she should try to secure.

"However, parents should not only set the standards but also provide the support and even the direct help the child needs when he or she doesn't meet these standards. This typically requires constant attention and communication, rather than only a monthly or yearly review of how well the child is doing in school."

A friend told me how he finally stopped being a poor student in grammar school and learned to concentrate on his studies. His father and mother enrolled him in a suburban Chicago private school called The North Shore School of Concentration. The school was run by a retired teacher in his home, and he managed to show amazing results in helping underachievers study better.

My friend, then about twelve, was having trouble with math in school. At the School of Concentration, the instructor set Bill down at a table with a math problem and simply told him to figure it out for himself, no matter how long it might take.

Bill stared at that problem for most of the first day and the second. On the third day, he suddenly looked up at the instructor and said, "Oh, I get it!" He completed the problem and, elated that he was able to think it out all by himself, instantly graduated from the school. He went on to become an above-average student when he returned to the regular school system.

This and other teaching methods are espoused today by many private schools to help underachieving young people, including the Institute for Motivational Development in Lombard, Illinois. Harry Davis, a spokesperson for the institute, says that there often is an emotional reason for a young person's poor performance in school.

"A child with an IQ of 124 is getting D's and F's on his report card and his excuse is, 'I can't concentrate,'" says Davis. "'My teacher and I have a personality conflict. The radiator next to my desk is too noisy.'

"One parent said, 'My son told me that he couldn't pay attention in class because it was during summer and as he was supposed to be preparing for a test, he was bothered by the noise of the custodian's lawn mower outside the window beside him.'

"When your child focuses on these issues and then you focus on them, you're not really going to deal with the problem. The real problem is a motivational block. It's almost as if the youngster is setting things up so he *doesn't* learn. He welcomes distractions and needs to have them as excuses for his lack of performance.

"At the institute we call it 'dependency seeking.'

The child is dependent on other situations supposedly outside his control as explanations for not doing well in school. These can get out of hand, in the example of an older boy who steals a car. He's caught by the police and his parents beg, 'Why did you do that?' And the boy says, 'Oh, I just took it for a joy ride. The guy who really is to blame is the guy who left his keys in the ignition.'

"In other words, the boy is saying, 'The focus of responsibility is something I don't have any control over,' or 'You deal with the other parties outside of me, and *then* maybe I'll perform.'

"Some of these kids are very good at concentrating. But they're concentrating on working out ways of getting out of a task as opposed to applying themselves to do it. I've been a teacher and a principal and now I'm a parent. I know more about what a parent and teacher can do to make sure a youngster has fewer distractions. You have to be careful that you don't set things up so youngsters feel that 'Mom and Dad and teachers are doing the worrying and the planning and, as long as *they're* doing that, making all the decisions for me, I don't have to!'

"In a sense, some kids *need* failure. They are more threatened by success than they are by failure. We're finding this typical of young people in the junior high to high school grades."

Davis says that some children's emotional blocks force them to do just about anything to keep from being responsible:

"When you've gone beyond all efforts to eliminate the supposed complaints and distractions your child

50

insists are keeping him from concentrating on his studies, and he still tries to weasel out of studying, he may sabotage any efforts you make to try to help him focus on concentrating. It often means the youngster is very directly going into an apppraoch of, 'How can I get out of this?, because if I am put into a situation where I really *have* to apply myself, that means I'm going to have to work and be responsible, and I'm going to try and dodge that.'

"When the usual tools don't seem to be productive enough in turning the child around, there can be an emotional block that the youngster finds himself in. Often, logic and power don't work with this type of youngster.

"When this happens, you're probably dealing with a youngster who has an emotional block. One of his fears may be, 'If I start performing, I'll be abandoned or ignored.'

"Oddly enough, the involvement that the parents have in their child's life, when the youngster is doing well enough to barely get by, is important enough to the children to keep it going.

"In severe cases we tell parents, in a tactful way, to withdraw from the youngster. Back off. Don't get too involved, and let the youngster be faced with the consequences of his own problems.

"The situation of the boy, Bill, who was ignored until he figured out the math problem for himself, is a healthy one. You simply tell the child, 'I'm not going to hover over you. I'm not going to lecture you. I'm just going to tell you that this is what has to be done, by this time. You're on your own.'

"A lot of kids will try to test that and throw the guilt feelings back onto Mom and Dad. But if the instructor is strong enough, the focus for helping the youngster concentrate can be a healthy sense of abandonment.

"You just tell him, 'Kid, I know you've got the ability. But you're on your own. Goodbye!'"

Dr. Linnus S. Pecaut, a psychologist who directs the Institute for Motivational Development, says some youngsters try so hard to do well that they fail. Others learn that succeeding only brings pressure for even better performance, and so find it easier to fail. Many realize that they receive more attention when they fail than when they succeed and are naturally reluctant to give up this attention.

"Many youngsters become underachievers and problems because the parent has become overinvolved in their lives," says Pecaut.

Students can be grouped into four distinct groups according to the developmental issue causing the interference with learning, says Pecaut. These are trust-seeking, approval-seeking, dependence-seeking, and independence-seeking. Treatment for each of these developmental problems is different and unique.

But some treatment is essential, Pecaut insists, since he believes that America's teenagers have subtly taken control of the two major social units in which they function — the school and the home.

"The roles have been reversed," Pecaut says, "so that society now seeks the approval of the child, rather than making the child earn the approval of society."

Meanwhile, educators have discovered that concentration in young people can no longer be regarded as a general power of the mind which, when developed in one subject, will be turned on any or all subjects with equal intensity.

Educators' fondest hopes for a mental discipline which would apply generally to all situations have been shattered by recent results of experiments on the transfer of training. It has been proven rather conclusively that no school subject is better than any other for developing reasoning, concentration, or general mind-training. A student's concentration may be good in one subject, but this does not mean that the student will concentrate equally well on another.

Concentration involves more than attitude, says Hopkins. A fundamental interest is vital to successful concentration, and so is motivation. It is the development of that interest which is the aim of the teacher. Motivation, Hopkins maintains, is the real essential in concentration.

"The fact is that you *can* concentrate," Hopkins says, "but most people have to be shown *why* they should."

Hopkins finds that a program of yoga, which tends to be a form of active relaxation, is effective in dissipating excess energy, and at the same time fosters concentration. Relaxation can lead to a more efficient approach to many tasks, and it imparts a feeling of well-being and calmness.

Hopkins says it is important to increase one's attention span. We must learn to finish one task before going on to another. We must make a set of priorities for the use of our time and energy.

One aid to better concentration, particularly before

taking an examination, making a speech, or conducting a class demonstration, is to visualize yourself in control of the situation beforehand. Imagine yourself to be completely confident, composed, relaxed, and completing the task in an easy manner.

Parents can help to foster better concentration and improved study by selecting truly educative activities for their children at a very early age. While this process of selection may help young people lead up to and prepare for the indispensable activities of adult life, it also finds sufficient justification in its present reflex influence upon the formation of orderly habits of thought.

From an early age, children must be helped to select acts and objects as means for reaching ends. With selection go arrangement and adaptation. These operations demand judgment. Suitable conditions work unconsciously to build up an attitude favorable to reflective operations. Games children are given to play, books they are directed to read, television shows and movies of educational value that they are encouraged to watch, can help them to form excellent habits of thought and to select acts and objects which can encourage concentration skills and better learning powers.

From the foregoing it is obvious that the parent and teacher must learn to determine when it is to the child's benefit to leave him to his own devices and when to guide him into directions which can help him toward greater concentration and achievement.

Every child's educational destiny is practically determined before he reaches school age, according to

Elizabeth Childe, a teacher and mother who became an authority on teaching concentration some years ago.

"There is no faculty more essential to scholarship than concentration," Ms. Childe has declared. "The ability to pay attention. And yet, ninety-nine children out of a hundred have the habit of inattention not only taught but drilled into them from the time they can toddle. When a mother calls her child at play and gets no response, and keeps calling without getting his attention and response, then gives up, she is reinforcing that child not to pay attention when asked to respond to any command. How could there be a more thorough training in inattention than some four or five years of this talking to heedless ears?"

Ms. Childe contends that almost everybody is capable of something like concentration when very deeply interested.

"The mind is all there, absorbed, active, alert. But it is only when this interest is controlled, and can be harnessed at will wherever it is needed, that we can rightly call it concentration. The habit of controlled interest or, better self-controlled interest, is a compound habit, the result of two simple habits both of which may, with a reasonable amount of persistence, be taught to any child.

"The first of these is *self-control*. It comes only through discipline, and is notoriously lacking in present-day American children. There is very little of the true spirit of obedience among our juvenile population, and what there seems to be is due for the most part to parental tact and diplomacy, not to the strength and firmness that beget genuine respect in the heart of a child.

"The second of these habits is that of being *habitually interested in everything that is unknown*. It comes from the right training of the normal curiosity with which all healthy children are blessed. But it is possible only where children have the inestimable privilege of the right sort of adult companionship — intimate, chummy adult companionship that visits and visits and visits about everything under the sun."

Ms. Childe says she makes these statements with some degree of confidence because the most remarkable power of concentration with which she has ever had dealings is one which she herself has trained according to those principles.

"An obedient spirit alone will not necessarily make children clever," says Ms. Childe. "But it is unquestionably the best possible foundation for mental development, because it is the teachable spirit.

"It also makes possible and pleasant the intimate adult companionship that is by far the most important element in education. There is no more delightful companion than a well-trained, obedient, teachable child, who fully realizes that his elders are in a position of authority over him, and that they actually do know more about most things than he does. And there is for such a child no other experience that begins to be so educational or so inspiring as the right sort of adult companionship, which is neither overindulgent nor condescending, but is always feeding and leading his God-given curiosity."

Young people enter college "badly damaged articles," says Ms. Childe, with no core of knowledge to which the facts they fumble with may cling, no keen-edged linguistic or scientific tools with which to cut to the heart of the matter, no memory trained and enriched, no taste, no imagination, no judgment balanced by frequent trial, no habits of remorseless application. They have bluffs but not confidence; they have promise but not power.

But she maintains that similarly, children enter high school just as "badly damaged articles," and so it goes all the way to children entering kindergarten. The damage, she contends, is done in the home.

"Lack of concentration, which is at the bottom of the whole trouble, does not mean, as many suppose, that concentration has merely not yet begun to grow," says Ms. Childe. "Lack of concentration is a bad habit of inattention that, like thumb-sucking, should never have been begun. And concentration is merely the firmly established habit of attention that should be understood by all parents, just as sanitation and infant hygiene should be understood.

"If we parents do not want our children to dawdle through their childhood, to hem and haw and make excuses, to spend a hour over ten minutes' worth of work or else shirk it altogether, *we must teach them to concentrate.*

"If we want them to have a 'core of knowledge to which facts may cling,' 'keen-edged tools with which to cut to the heart of the matter;' if we want them to have confidence instead of bluff, and power as well as promise, we must teach them to concentrate. The earlier we begin, the better we will succeed.

"Some educators have laid the responsibility for faulty training upon the home. But they maintain that educators must find the remedy and educate the parents. However, they believe that to wait for the home to become what it should be, would be to wait until there is no further need of education.

"They may be right, but I am convinced that for the parents to wait to be educated by the educators would be for us to wait until our children's grandchildren are past the need of education. It seems a pity to wait so long."

Interestingly enough, the children Ms. Childe referred to are already grandparents because it may surprise you to know, she wrote those thoughts on concentration in 1915.

The most common complaints students have, especially in high school and college, revolve around their inability to concentrate during a study or testing session. Acts of willpower and fear-arousing talk ("I've got to get this right or I'll fail!") are the most common methods they use to cope with distractions, frustration, and fatigue.

But these methods are at best only partially effective and share in the drawback of putting the student under considerable tension. The tension probably adds subsequent negative feelings about entering into the next study or testing session. It is a vicious circle which only reinforces bad studying habits and contributes to even greater loss of concentration.

There are better ways of increasing your powers of concentration in school and, of course, they can be applied to concentrating better on any task or challenge that comes up at home or in your work life.

It seems appropriate here to include a quotation on this subject from F. Scott Fitzgerald, who once wrote:

"The test of a first-rate intelligence is the ability to hold two opposed ideas in the mind at the same time, and still retain the ability to function. One should, for example, be able to see that things are hopeless and yet be determined to make them otherwise."

For starters, let's take advantage of the thoughts on concentration generously offered to the author by Professor Dean Trembly, head of the Testing and Counseling Center of California Polytechnic State University in San Luis Obispo, California. Professor Trembly believes he knows the formula for greater concentration:

"Imagination is the prime mover, the driving power, the intrinsic motivator behind divergent, creative production. Those with an over-abundance of ideas can take one thing and weave around it many implications. Variety is an ever-present need; restlessness is an ever-present annoyance when the aptitude is not fully used in a constructive way."

To concentrate and study better, Ralph Preston, a Chicago educator and author of *How to Study*, suggests:

"Rid yourself of anxiety and tension, especially those resulting from internal personal conflicts.

"An important part of our instructional program [in better concentration and study techniques] is 'the mastery technique,' which emphasizes active reading through searching for answers to self-formulated questions, and note-taking to aid retention.

"The use of this *active mind* of reading and studying

helped students to improve their ability to concentrate because they provided themselves with specific purposes and goals for their studying, rather than aimless meandering through the content."

Preston suggests that students *not* underline words in their study materials. Instead, *write down* key words and sentences in note form on a separate sheet of paper or in a notebook.

Using key words helps to summarize the material to be learned, so you can focus your attention on the "meat" of the material. It also helps, Preston says, if you *say* the key words or sentences to yourself.

"If you read a few pages of a text and can't grasp the material; if your mind wanders," says Preston, "formulate *questions* and look for *answers* in the text. If you know what you're looking for, it will jump out at you from the page."

Lois Lynn Hardy, who has done extensive research into how to improve studying in high school, has some recommendations for improving your study conditions which can be applied by anyone of any age. They all add up to greater concentration in study.

Work at a desk or table with a surface large enough that you can spread out your work. Do not use a bed for study. Keep a bookshelf or table close to your desk, to set books and other reference material on. Pen, pencil, dictionary, paper, books, and other study materials should be close at hand.

Find a quiet place to study. It is not possible to study in the same room where a television set is on, because you cannot concentrate on your studying and tune in to a television show at the same time. Also don't expect to get much or any studying done if friends are present. Talking and laughing will kill your concentration on studying. The quieter the place for study, the fewer the distractions, the better your concentration will be.

Avoid interruptions. If you have trouble keeping others, such as pestering brothers or sisters, out of your study area at home, maybe you should not study at home, but perhaps at the library, where you can cut out more distractions and interruptions. If you must study at home, the family should arrange for rules about receiving telephone calls or visitors during study time.

Study under a good light. It should be bright enough (100 watts is the minimum brightness for study), well-distributed (diffused) so there is no glare, and the light should be placed so that it doesn't shine into your eyes.

The National Society for the Prevention of Blindness reports that only about 5 percent of students tested were found to study under those three minimum lighting requirements. The society maintains that good lighting not only protects your eyes, it helps reduce study fatigue.

If your study light does produce glare, place it behind you, or bounce the light off a wall. And never study with a single lamp over your books, with the rest of the room dark. There must be another source of light in the room to protect your eyes.

Keep your study room on the cool side. A few degrees on the cool side of 70 degrees will keep you more alert than if you study in a room that is too warm, which may overly relax you and make you drowsy. Also be sure the room is adequately ventilated. Some fresh air circulating in the room will help you keep your mind clear.

Assume good posture while studying. Sit in a chair that is comfortable, but not *too* comfortable. Do not expect to get much studying done if you lie on a couch or slouch in a beanbag chair. A firm chair with good back support can help you to improve your concentration and therefore to study better.

Get into a mood for study. Even if you don't feel much like studying, don't put it off until you might get into the mood. Once you start to study, you will find that the mood to study will come upon you if you give it any chance at all. Setting up your study area, choosing the books you will be looking at, or simply opening up one of them can help create the mood for study. If you get into a habit of quickly settling down to work, it will help you to control your study mood.

Study at a regular time and place, every day. This also will help create a habit for studying. Besides, it also saves time, since you will be able to block out an hour or two for study all at one time and get more out of it than if you scattered your studying in shorter intervals throughout the day.

Study at the right time of day. It is harder to study after a heavy meal or after vigorous exercise when you may feel too relaxed or even groggy. Perhaps the best time to study is before going to sleep at night. Your study then will be especially effective, since tests have shown that sleeping after study increases retention. But don't use this as an excuse to sleep in class!

Take some study breaks. Although some students can study effectively for two hours without taking a rest break, most people need a break at least after an hour's study, especially those with reading problems. Somewhat shorter periods of concentrated study are recommended for them — perhaps twenty minutes, followed by a short break.

Most of us can benefit from a short rest break after working or studying for more than two or three ours. A stretch, walk around the room, taking deep breaths, limbering up, can help refresh our bodies and minds. Just be sure to keep the rest breaks short. In Japan, workers take "breathing breaks." Every fifteen minutes they stop work and inhale and exhale deeply. In addition to relaxing them, the increased oxygen intake can help them think and work better.

The foregoing study conditions can be very important. Ms. Hardy warns that the lack of them — being faced with noise, poor light, inadequate study space, and frequent interruptions — will force you to study that much harder to overcome the distractions that are created.

Concentration may sound like hard work to most of us, but it doesn't really have to be. We can usually concentrate on things that really interest us. Take the eventful day when American astronauts first walked on the moon. Millions of people in all parts of the world concentrated intensely during that historic event, following the activities of the astronauts from blast-off to moon walk. Many people gave up their sleep to tune in on the live televised reports as they came to us by satellite in all parts of the world. We didn't have any trouble concentrating on the moon walk because we were intensely *interested* in it.

Since it is *interest* which induces effortless concentration, and conversely since lack of interest is the basic cause of the inability to concentrate, it is of the utmost importance that we find out what it is that creates interest.

Another researcher into concentration and learning, Dr. Bruno Furst, says interest, in its broadest sense, is reward. "Reward" can have many different meanings for different people, ranging from financial gain to the intellectual satisfaction of acquiring knowledge.

If you take a self-improvement course in memory training, for example, you look forward to the reward of being able to remember better. The ability to remember will be rewarding in many ways, including better study or job performance and consequently, higher grades or better pay.

If you enroll in a computer-programming course you will be able to concentrate on your studies because you realize that a direct result of learning well will be greater job opportunity. You may earn promotions to higher levels of computer study, become a systems analyst, and climb further up the ladder of success.

But most often, says Furst, the relationship between effort (concentration) and result (reward) is not so immediately visible.

Students who have problems studying often complain that if they could skip the subjects they hate, they would do well in school. Why take biology when the student wants to be a jet pilot? Educators and parents try to answer this query by persuading the young person that he or she needs "an education." In order to get this education, it isn't enough to get passing grades in just the subjects you like or are interested in, subjects which may come quite easily for you. Once you accept that it is to your ultimate benefit to study a wider range of subjects than only those you like, you have taken your first step toward walking on a moon of your own. With a better attitude toward your studies, you put in a little extra effort. The little extra concentration you bring to your study or to a task nearly always results in a realization that the subject material is not as hard to digest as you thought.

Encouragement is very important, says Furst. And not so much from parents or teachers, but most importantly, the encouragement that comes from tasting the gratifying sense of success in having done something correctly or well.

Students can draw strength from this gratifying sense of accomplishment. It puts a lot more determination into a student's attitude. Now he can give his studies the needed concentration. More comprehension, better remembering, is only a natural result from this greater concentration.

But there are distractions that come from *within*, Furst advises us. Some of us may start to concentrate on a subject or task with the best intentions, but after a short while, our minds wander in any and all directions.

Dr. Furst believes that the method many people use for memorizing information is to blame for this distraction from within. Too often, people try to "hammer" material into their heads by parrotlike repetition, over and over again. Furst believes it is a pity that learning by rote is still the most universally practiced method of memorizing.

The reasoning behind repetition in learning is that if a little repetition is good, then a great deal of repetition must be better. But Furst says that the results should have proved this reasoning to be entirely wrong. Constant, humdrum repetition, he believes, is the very cause of mind-wandering.

A more effective study method is to study, learn, and remember by way of association, Furst contends. Association stimulates the mind. If we learn to think in pictures, our study material becomes colorful — and so much more eagerly absorbed by our minds! Then we need much less repetition to make it our mental property.

Imagination should be given free rein, says Furst, because it is boundless imagination that makes learning pleasure instead of drudgery. Imaginative visualization can make the most difficult text material easy to digest, since it induces concentration and widens our attention span to a previously unthinkable degree.

It isn't only in the field of study that concentration should be diligently practiced, Furst declares. We could do well with a healthy dose of concentration as we conduct our everyday lives. In our conversations with others, how much more misunderstanding would be avoided if we concentrated a little harder on what the other person was trying to say? How often do we even let the other person finish what he wants to say to us before we try to cut him off or take an opposing view?

Older people returning to school, such as senior citizens enrolling in courses to complete high school or college, may encounter mental blocks toward concentrating on their studies. They may invent countless chores which they tell themselves must be attended to before they can study their school assignment. Like a youngster without a parent to make him sit and study, an older person may put off study until the next day, and then the day after that.

This procrastination, say Melvin Powers and Robert S. Starrett, researchers of study and concentration, should be recognized for what it is — elderly people's fear that they will not be able to concentrate or learn at their advanced age. If this fear is not overcome, they may give up the course of study, using lack of time as the excuse. But the decision they *should* reach is that *nothing* should interfere with their study routine. If we are honest with ourselves, at any age, we will admit that there are seldom real emergencies which can interfere with our study.

Powers' and Starrett's theories on the proper length of time to devote to uninterrupted study differ from that of other researchers. In the first stages of learning how to concentrate, they say, it is likely that half an hour will be as long as the mind can fix its attention before wandering. Later on, an hour or longer will not be too difficult. They suggest a short rest period will always enable you to return to your work with renewed zest.

Emotional and physical problems can prevent the

mind from concentrating on a text. People who attempt to read under stress may read entire chapters without remembering a single word or thought. If these problems become aggravated to the extent that it is impossible to fix attention on anything, they require professional attention, just as much as improper vision. While tests are now uncovering these problems in young people, adults must discover their emotional and physical problems themselves if these interfere with their powers of concentration.

Better concentration, reading, and learning can all be improved, says Powers and Starrett, if we tune in to the many different ways there are of reading.

Memorizing math formulas or historical dates requires different reading methods than those applied to philosophy or literature. Some books are written so you can skim through them very quickly, absorbing only the salient facts and still gaining sufficient comprehension. Reading technical material requires more detailed study, and learning a foreign language may require complete attention to every word.

Before reading a book, it is important to consider the purpose of the book and to study its table of contents. Often the jacket or forword will clue you in to how completely you should read the book. Just skimming through a book can give you a great deal of information on how much you should concentrate on particular chapters.

Skimming through a book is best done if you want to find specific answers to specific questions. Sometimes just a quick glance at a page can tell you that the answer you seek is not in that part of the book.

If your object is to form a critical judgment of an author's ideas, reading at a slower pace is necessary. While reading you must put your mind through logical thought processes to decide whether the ideas or theories are valid or invalid. You must constantly compare what you know about the subject with what the author is saying.

Powers and Starrett suggest that the objective of all reading which has learning as its goal is thought stimulation. As you read, you should continually ask yourself how the information being obtained can fit into your own plan of learning. Along similar lines, they maintain that comprehension and speed in reading are linked closely. If your comprehension is good, you seldom will need to reread a sentence in order to understand its meaning. But poor readers must continually return to earlier material, which slows down their reading considerably. In complicated material, however, even good readers may have to regress some before they completely understand what they are reading. Hopefully, their concentration improves rather than diminishes with each rereading.

Attention and concentration in reading can be improved with practice. When practice reading, always read at a rate that is faster than your normal reading speed. Don't go back and reread material while practice reading. If you think you've missed some meaning, reread it from the beginning for a second time. Then you will find you can comprehend all the ideas at the faster rate of speed.

Really fast readers who still attain comprehension of the material are successful skim-readers. They may actually read only one sentence in a paragraph, or even just one sentence on a page. They have mastered the technique of looking for information clues which they can identify as important to the total theme of the material they are reading. But this should only be done when you are reading in order to find the answer to a specific question or questions.

In trying to read faster, remember not to force your speed to the point where comprehension suffers. Test your speed-reading by first reading some material at a rapid pace, and then seeing if you can write down on paper the important points.

Do this both immediately upon reading the material and also again, about an hour later. If you can't remember most of the important points in your reading, it means you probably are reading too fast. Slow down until your comprehension matches your speed.

But Powers and Starrett remind us that this technique only applies to material you must learn for study purposes. For reading practice sessions, reading faster than you can comprehend can be good, because they contend that comprehension will gradually catch up with speed. You simply force your mind to learn faster.

These techniques for acquiring greater concentration and comprehension while reading faster only work if you are strongly motivated and practice every day. You will be rewarded with greater self-esteem when you find you are able to understand everything you read at a faster rate. This will enable you to read more and more difficult material.

While it is true that some subjects are more fun

than others, and some instructors are better than others, some students are able to tune in to both their material and their teachers. Often the reason is that these students have set long-range goals for themselves. They "have their act together." No matter how difficult the subject or how much they may dislike or disagree with the instructor, they know that a particular subject is a hurdle they have to get over because it is one stepping-stone in their journey toward becoming what they want to be — doctor, lawyer, whatever.

These students are able to concentrate on difficult or less-pleasant subjects because they view all their courses as means to an end. Goals are powerful motivators.

Daydreaming is another common complaint among students having concentration problems in class. Psychologists tell us that a certain amount of daydreaming — a way of living our life in fantasy — can be extremely beneficial, if it is not carried too far and the fantasies are within the scope of our abilities.

But when daydreaming interferes with a serious task, it usually means we are not interested in the task and are trying to avoid the reality of the situation. If we daydream while studying subjects which are necessary to our future success, we are probably not strongly enough motivated. In this case, we should give some thought to whether the goal we have set for ourselves is realistic.

Some final words seem in order here on health. We can concentrate better if we are healthy, though intense concentration can even help us forget we are in physical pain. If you are in good health, you should be able to concentrate on a task. Keep both your body and mind healthy. Get adequate exercise and sleep.

Drugs interfere with or prevent us from concentrating. Alcohol and marijuana don't mix well with study. The same applies for the harder drugs. Tobacco also is bad for concentration because it constricts the blood vessels and cuts down on oxygen to the brain.

Proper nutrition helps the brain to function better. Oysters and rare roast beef are said to be good aids to concentration. Vitamin B-12, glutamic acid, and niacin (nicotinic acid) are all brain vitamins. They help to nourish the brain.

Liver, brewer's yeast, and pumpkin seeds high in zinc are other good brain-concentration foods. Green vegetables are helpful, and meat supplies folic acid which is a synthetic form of one of the B complex of vitamins.

Choline, a food substance found in egg yolks, meat, and fish, reportedly has a strong impact on the brain's ability to produce acetylcholine. This important neurochemical improves the memory according to Dr. Richard J. Wurtman, a specialist in neuro-endocrine regulation at the Massachusetts Institute of Technology.

Food for thought for older people may involve taking more of certain nutrients than younger people, especially vitamin B-12, which helps combat anemia and fights off senility.

Sometimes, weather conditions can seriously interfere with our ability to concentrate. Hot, humid days can sap our energy so we can't think well. Air pollution also takes its toll on our powers of concentration.

Among the worst offenders among air pollutants is ozone.

Ozone is a pungent, colorless, highly toxic gas that irritates and inflames the walls of the air passages and increases the work of breathing. This places a strain on the heart and lungs and interferes with our ability to concentrate and to cope with even minor mental tasks or problems.

During hot, sunny days with stagnant air, automobile exhaust fumes and other ozone-creators take their toll on our mental powers. We may find it almost impossible to concentrate on our work. During ozone alerts, if you cannot work in air-conditioned or other air-purified places, it may be best to put off demanding tasks until the air clears in a few hours or days. Athletes and children are especially cautioned not to take part in strenuous exercise during ozone alerts, which can permanently damage the lungs and heart.

But ozone and other air pollutants aside, the general rule is to concentrate on developing good health, primarily through proper diet and sufficient exercise, and to avoid those things which can sap your energy and enthusiasm or adversely alter your thinking. Good health and concentration go hand in hand.

5

How to Concentrate Better at Work

Part of the ceiling in the operating room of a Chicago hospital fell one day during surgery. But the surgeon was concentrating so intently on the operation he was performing that only afterward did he ask a nurse what all the plaster was doing on the floor around the operating table.

This story is told by Mihaly Csikszentmihalyi, a University of Chicago psychologist who is an authority on concentration.

"When we are involved in activities that are rewarding in and of themselves," says "Dr. C.," "a feeling emerges which I call *flow*. It is an elementary reward we get in everything we consider to be 'enjoyment.' It can be described as the 'fun' in fun.

"Flow occurs when — like the surgeon — we are completely immersed in what we are doing. In this state, we lose a self-conscious sense of ourselves and of time. We achieve a heightened awareness of our physical involvement with an activity.

"The person in flow finds, among other things, that his concentration vastly increases and his feedback from the activity is enormously enhanced. In flow, you are in an ecstatic state to such a point that you don't exist."

Dr. C. says that when you are in flow, you undergo an itense centering of attention on whatever activity or job you are performing. You don't necessarily try to concentrate harder — the concentration comes automatically. As an expert chess player described his flow, "The game is a struggle, but the concentration is like breathing. You never think of it." A dancer says, "You are totally involved in what you are doing. Your body feels good and is awake all over. Your energy is flowing very smoothly. You feel relaxed, comfortable, and energetic."

"There is a merging of action and awareness in the period of flow," says Dr. C. "It is a floating action in which you may be aware of your actions but not be aware of your awareness. There is a sense of being lost in the action. Time passes a hundred times faster, like in a dream state."

Our attitudes toward our work could be altered for the better by achieving flow, Dr. C. reports. Too many people are bored with their jobs, discontented and alienated by their work. Putting flow into work would enrich the worker's life.

To help bring flow into our work, to achieve the centering of attention necessary to allow flow to happen to us in whatever activity we are performing, Dr. C. suggests that a preliminary ritual is necessary. He likens this ritual to that of a priest who, before Mass, dons his vestments and murmurs prayers to block out distractions and focus his thoughts on the Mass he is about to celebrate.

Similarly, football and hockey players are performing a preliminary ritual when they mutter curses as they put on their safety pads and other equipment before a game. Musicians are performing a ritual when they tune up their instruments before a concert. Sculptors knead their clay before starting work. Baseball players put dirt or resin on their hands before picking up a bat, and take a few warm-up swings to get their minds on swatting the ball. A pitcher may work the ball over in his hands, getting the feel for the ball and getting his mind on his pitching before tossing out the first pitch.

"It is possible to flow while engaged in any activity," says Dr. C. "We can achieve it in our work and our daily lives." He recommends five basic steps toward achieving flow, which he says can help show us how to achieve greater concentration:

1. *Fit difficulty to skill.* A requisite for flow is an even match between the difficulty of a challenge and our ability to meet it. If the demands are too slight, we feel bored. If the demands are too great, we feel anxious.

2. *Focus attention.* Some people can achieve flow simply by focusing their attention to allow the merging of awareness and activity. Any activity can spark flow if we focus well enough on it.

3. *Forget time.* We can flow in any activity if we are in the right frame of mind. Things can flow if we focus on the moment, so that we can respond to feedback from the immediate situation. To do this, lay aside thoughts of the past or plans for the future. Preoccupation with, or worries about, what we have to do next or what we have just done interferes with the immediate activity. This frame of mind takes us out of the

moment so we lose flow. Flow exists only in the present.

4. *Relax and wake up.* Let go of worrisome concerns. Relax. But stay alert. Become fully aware of what is happening in the immediate situation. Notice what your body is doing.

"The domain of flow is the band between anxiety and boredom," says Dr. C. "An alert mind resists boredom by keeping us involved in events around us. A relaxed body is the physiological opposite of tension. The two together — alert mind and relaxed body — combine to make us ripe for flow.

5. *Training for flow.* Any discipline that focuses us on the here and now brings us closer to flow. Dance and some Eastern martial arts combine awareness and movement to center attention. Certain meditation techniques instill mindfulness, the ability to focus on whatever is happening at the moment, no matter what it may be.

Unfortunately, not all of us are able to work in jobs that are rewarding in and of themselves. Those who work in some of the time-honored professions — doctors, lawyers, teachers, musicians, artists, writers —can often achieve high levels of concentration and also enjoy what they are doing. They get so wrapped up in work that is pleasurable to them that concentration comes easily.

One of the greatest enemies of concentration is noise. Noise, which seems to be in greater abundance in our lives every year, has been an annoyance and detractor from concentration for a long, long time.

Julius Caesar complained of noise in 44 B.C. when

he wrote the first anti-noise ordinance. Two centuries later, the noise in Rome was still so great, a senator complained, "It is absolutely impossible to sleep anywhere in the city. The perpetual traffic of wagons in the streets is sufficient to wake the dead!"

Alas, eighteen centuries later we are still suffering from noise pollution worse than ever. Our offices and factories are becoming so noisy and full of distractions that it often is almost impossible to concentrate on any task, whether we are working at a desk or on an assembly line.

I pleaded with my boss at the big insurance company where I was editor of the external travel magazine for the motor club:

"You've got me working in a room with metal walls and huge glass windows. Sounds bounce around here like tenpins in a bowling alley.

"Eight of us share the room, with electric typewriters clattering, telephones jangling, dictation machines jibber-jabbering. And the traffic flow of people coming and going around here makes this place as bad as Grand Central Station!

"I need a room I can *think* in, that I can *concentrate* in! I'll settle for a cubicle, not even a room with four walls and a ceiling. Get me out of this squirrel cage, so I can get some work done!"

Of course all my complaints fell on deaf ears. Corporations today don't believe in environments conducive to effective working or concentrating. They believe in some sort of "family of workers" which makes them push everyone together into a small area where we all have to somehow cope with each other's noise. We are all supposed to get along better because we are in closer contact with each other.

But instead of getting along better at desks lined up in rows and rows, most modern workers find they can hardly function. Noise and other distractions take their toll not only on productivity, but on our nervous systems. Most modern office workers are put in work situations no better than the crowded, noisy conditions in factories, yet they are expected to think and concentrate on what they're doing.

Noise in the workplace has become the most prevalent hazard faced by employees, whether white-collar or blue-collar, and both the federal government and industry are dragging their feet on efforts to protect the hearing of workers, says Dr. Maurice H. Miller, professor of audiology at New York University.

Besides loss of concentration, an estimated 16.5 million American workers already have suffered significant hearing loss because of job-related noise damage. The hearing loss ranges from mild to severe, but the worst part about it is that the loss is permanent. Dramatic as that figure is, no figures are yet available on the effect noise and other workplace distractions have on our ability to concentrate, or their affect on our peace of mind.

"Noise doesn't kill, but it is the great destroyer of the quality of life," says Dr. Miller. "It can prevent a worker from hearing his children at play, a bird sing, going to an outdoor concert, or being able to communicate."

Every day, 37.5 million workers in this country are exposed to potentially hazardous noise levels at their jobs. There are five million work areas in which noise levels are dangerous. Hearing loss is insidious because it is painless and gradual and most workers don't even know it's happening to them.

Only about 5 to 10 percent of the companies with noise hazards have acted in any way to protect their workers. Some industries are requiring special headgear or earplugs to meet state noise standards. In some other companies, noise levels have been brought down by modifications of machines and work areas, according to manufacturers' spokesmen.

The federal government has been proposing to limit noise exposure levels for workers to ninety decibels per eight-hour period in order to prevent hearing damage. This level is equivalent to the sound of a subway train as it pulls into a station. One hundred decibels is equivalent to the noise made by ten trains pulling in.

The economic crunch the nation has experienced for several years is not helping industry solve its noise pollution problems. Many experts believe it would be safer to limit workplace noise to eighty-five decibels, but it would cost $18.5 billion to bring industry into compliance. The U.S. Chamber of Commerce estimates that the cost of lowering noise levels to eighty-five decibels would range as high as $32 billion.

About 80 million Americans, according to an Environmental Protection Agency report, live in areas in which the ambient sound often is loud enough to interfere with speech. Out of these, 40 million have to tolerate sound levels that threaten their hearing, and one out of twenty people suffer some hearing loss.

This noise not only reduces the quality of city life, it can impair mental and physical health. And things aren't growing better. Ambient city noises are increasing a half-decibel a year.

Dr. Thomas H. Fay, director of speech and hearing at Columbia-Presbyterian Medical Center in New York, explains the multifaceted results of ear pollution, at home or in the city or workplace:

"Hearing loss is far less of a problem than the erosion of the quality of life for the millions of people who have to put up with intolerable noise levels. Loud and ubiquitous city noise and the stress it produces are probably causing all kinds of physical and emotional problems we don't even know about yet."

Dr. Barbara A. Bohne, a professor at Washington University in St. Louis, believes that one reason noise has become a problem is that the ear is now subjected to sounds which evolution did not prepare it for. Originally, the ear was apparently intended to detect soft sounds that usually signaled danger or food, and then to trigger the body's fight-or-flight mechanism. But today, though most sounds no longer are threatening to man, the ear mechanism is part and parcel of the human body and cannot be turned off.

So hearing a sound sets off a nervous reaction not unlike an anxiety attack, Dr. Bohne reports. Adrenalin is injected into the blood, the heart speeds up, blood vessels constrict, muscles tense, pupils dilate, and the stomach suffers brief spasms. Prolonged exposure to high levels of sound can even cause fluttering of the heart.

Sometimes, workers react rather violently to noise

they encounter on the job. The reason, say researchers at the National Institute of Mental Health, may be that people accustomed to high ambient noise have a more pronounced physical reaction to sudden noise than people who are used to more quiet. City people, therefore, are more apt to suddenly snap when they hear a loud sound.

In New York City, a man reacted so violently to a sudden loud noise in the sanitation department that he upended a man making the noise and pushed him into a trash barrel. A woman threatened the foreman of a noisy construction site with a shotgun. A man recently ran amok in a cafe in Mexico City, killing five people. In each case, the violent action was blamed on noise.

Unfortunately, our urban life is not getting quieter. It is predicted that if urban noises continue to increase at their present rate, by the start of the next century in less than twenty years, the cities will be twice as loud as they·are now.

So, when the noise and distraction conditions grew intolerable at my office, I quit. I was starting to get the shakes in the coffee break line even before I had any coffee. I decided it was time to get out of there and let the noisemakers do their things in the office squirrel cage, but without me. Later, to my sadness, I learned that one of the worst noise offenders in the office suffered a mental breakdown. I didn't think it was coincidence and marveled that there weren't more such cases from that abominable working environment.

How wonderful it feels, getting *that* off my mind and out of my system, after ten years! And I didn't even have to name the offending company. But if you write to me, I will.

So the problem in the workplace that keeps us from concentrating and probably even remotely enjoying our work, much less being productive or creative enough for promotion, is a combination of noise and distraction. How can we fight back, if we aren't able to throw up our hands and quit? Luckily, researchers have been thinking on the problem. Here are offered some solutions.

Probably the basic solution to tuning out noises and distractions interfering with our concentration at work is to achieve a higher level of interest in what we are doing.

A surgeon, when asked whether he really enjoyed his work, replied: "Like everyone else, I dislike some of the things I have to do. But when I operate, I lose all sense of time. I guess that's one way of gauging how much my work engrosses me."

The surgeon's report does tend to point up some of the cardinal requisites of concentration on the job. Not only interest and enjoyment, but skill and performance are called into play if we are to achieve high levels of concentration at work. If we can shut out other thoughts and noises or distractions while we work at a particular task, we are sure to be able to do the job better and enjoy our work more. Satisfaction with job performance also can reinforce concentration, because we all like to contemplate a success.

It is likely that the person who is easily distracted from his main tasks should consider the possibility that he is running away from dissatisfaction with his own efforts at work.

One thing each of us must try to achieve is a working atmosphere that helps us to concentrate better on our job and which hopefully can make the work go more pleasantly and be more personally satisfying and rewarding. It isn't an easy task, but if we follow all or at least some of the following recommendations, we should be able to achieve some good results.

Often the trick is knowing how to keep your mind on your work. Most researchers believe that it is not necessary to work in an environment of absolute silence. Some people prefer it, most people think they could concentrate best if they had it, but the fact is that many people work at least as well when they are exposed to steady or recurrent background noise. It could be soft music, which many factories and offices have been playing for years, or even the rumble of machinery, so long as it isn't too loud.

But most people work best when they stick to *predictable* sounds. We can actually become accustomed to most sounds (not noises), but we tend to work best when no unpredictable sounds or happenings distract us. Unexpected sounds or noises not only interfere with our concentration and thought processes, but such sounds also can impair our performance at the time we hear them and for some time afterward. Unexpected sounds at work tend to lower our capacity for good performance and our ability to withstand frustration, which is one of the great concentration-killers.

You may personally hate the antiseptic sound of Muzak and the other "used car showroom" types of light popular music your factory's or office's personnel department pipes through the loudspeaker system. But it may be preferable to the more distracting sounds that it tends to drown out.

Some years ago, tests were made in which mathematical puzzles, some solvable and some not, were given to people who were not aware of that fact. The point of the test was not to determine how accurately people solved the puzzles, but how persistently each person worked despite his or her frustration with the difficulty of the unsolvable problems.

One group of those tested was also exposed to a series of predictable noises. They did just about as well as those who worked on the puzzles in an atmosphere of complete silence. But those who had to study the puzzles under the pressure of unpredictable sounds showed a sharp drop in their ability to concentrate and in their patience to continue the test.

An executive of a major oil company where the tests were given says that the results confirmed what he always felt about the way a mind works, or at least the way his works:

"It always seems to me that my head must be like a telephone switchboard," he says. "It has only so many plugs and wires. But it is different in one respect from the switchboard. The fewer the lines in use, the louder and clearer each communication is.

"I can plug in on several currents of thought at once, if I have to. For instance, a little meeting can be going on in my office, and I can take an occasional phone call, okay a telex message, and sign a couple of urgent letters while half-hearing the conversation going on around my desk.

"However, their words are a little less meaningful. I get the main thoughts, but not the nuances that indicate how strongly each person feels on certain points. And I am sure that my ability to check the letters I sign is less precise.

"Also, just as this study shows, the distraction is much less if I get an expected and routine phone call than if an unexpected problem is tossed at me."

Another aid to better concentration at work is to try to keep to yourself for at least part of the work day, if possible. We benefit greatly if we can put up some "do not disturb" signs in our daily work schedule.

In most companies, trying to be alone for part of the day presents both practical and interpersonal problems. A closed door in an office or cubicle generally is regarded as an antisocial maneuver. I often tried to avoid lunching in the cafeteria or even taking traditional morning and afternoon coffee breaks, preferring to read a chapter of a book during that break period while all alone in an unused conference room at the unnamed insurance company. Most of my fellow workers tolerated my "eccentricity," but my supervisors considered my behavior little short of anarchy. I was "rocking the boat" by wanting to be off by myself to recharge my batteries with silence. I was not fitting in with the squirrel-cage environment the personnel department thought was best for everyone.

In most offices, it is considered impolite or antisocial to keep your door closed at all, much less for fifteen minutes or half an hour. The old and friendly idea that "my door is always open" has become very firmly entrenched in the business world so that a closed door indicates you are aloof or uncooperative. All it really means is that you need and desire a short period in which you can be by yourself, to restore your mental energy so you can handle the rest of the day.

Some forward-thinking companies allow certain employees to work at home, part or all of at least one day a week, if their jobs can permit such a schedule. Working at home for even half a day can result in greater productivity than one or more full days at the office, provided the concentration possibilities at home are better than those at the office. If the children are at school, for example, you may have enough quiet at home to accomplish a great deal of work. Other companies allow certain employees to go home a few hours early if they can finish their work better at home.

Many businessmen believe that the mere possibility that they will be interrupted at work reduces their ability to concentrate at the office, even if no interruption occurs.

One executive finds that he gets more work done and concentrates better if he takes an overnight train to his meeting destination, instead of an airplane that could get him there much sooner. He has found that only on a night train does he achieve the peak mental keenness he reaches after he closes himself into his train compartment. He knows that there he is totally out of contact with anyone who might intrude on his privacy.

"Train rattles, whistles, braking at stations, people walking by outside in the corridor . . . these are just a blur of sound that doesn't really come into my space," he says. "Since I don't have to do anything about them, I don't put the information through my mental computer."

Making war on clutter is another aid to concentration on the job. Visual as well as auditory distractions are killers of concentration.

Most work can be done best in an area that is free of clutter. People who think they can work well with a desk and office scattered with papers, books, old coffee cups, etc., are just fooling themselves. They should try working without clutter sometime and see the results.

Even a successful corporate lawyer who works in offices always cluttered with stacks of file folders and documents admitted once to a close friend, "I would like to be a Trappist monk and live in a bare cell!"

More on eliminating clutter from our work lives is discussed in chapter nine on organizing our work time and materials.

One of the main aids to good concentration on the job is adequate preparation. How we approach our work can determine how it will end up, just as the way a golfer addresses the ball so often foretells the fate of his shot.

If you start your work project with built-in distractions, such as intermittent questions to colleagues or visits to the file room, you are sure to be distracted. You may think that it is best to just get the business started and then see what questions arise as you go along, but this usually is very unproductive.

It may take some hard mental work to think through what the whole task will involve, to see in advance the order and nature of questions that will

89

arise in a work project, but it is less work in the end. The quality of the whole job also will be upgraded.

Before you start the project, get yourself as interested in it as you possibly can. Think of the positive aspects of successfully completing the project at hand. What will you gain from its success, financially or in other ways?

With some people, fear is the spur toward greater concentration.

Glenda Jackson, twice winner of the Academy Award for best motion picture actress, kindly wrote the author that:

"Unfortunately, I have no set techniques which enable me to achieve greater concentration. As far as work is concerned, it has always been my experience that fear is a great aid to concentrating the mind."

What Miss Jackson was referring to was apparently a fear of failure, of not performing a part in a way that measures up to her standards, or a fear of not interpreting a role properly.

In some crisis work situations, fear can be an important impetus toward greater concentration. On the one hand, there is supreme satisfaction at having reached a solution to a work problem or goal. On the other hand there is fear of the responsibility it imposes.

If you don't think fear is a valid tool to aid concentration, how about the fact that everyone concentrates if he is compelled to do so by the strength of self-preservation? Danger is a great incentive to concentration. The stock investor who receives an urgent message from his broker concentrates on the broker's danger warning about buying or selling. If the investor doesn't concentrate on the broker's message, he could be a heavy loser. A test-car driver for a motor company concentrates on his driving because he knows that if he doesn't, he may be killed on the test track.

One psychologist says that we are more liable to stray when walking on a wide road than when walking on the edge of a precipice. The difficulty is to concentrate voluntarily and to acquire concentration as a habit of mind.

Though fear is a viable concentration enhancer, it is generally suggested that it be the lesser motivation. Interest and positive attitude about success through good concentration should be easier for most of us, and more beneficial, with a little imagination.

Another concentration enhancer is relaxation. The one thing common to all forms of successful thinking is a peaceful mind. Stress and other factors that fatigue and distract always drag down our powers of concentration on the job.

The best cure for stress is rest or sleep. Adding an extra half-hour or hour to your normal sleep time is almost certain to make a healthy difference in how your mind operates. If possible, a midday nap can work similar wonders for clearing the mind.

If sleeping longer or taking a nap is impossible, try taking a walk. A brisk or fast walk is recommended rather than a leisurely stroll. It can improve blood circulation and sharpen the mind. On your next work day, try skipping the coffee on break and taking a brisk walk instead. It will get you out of the office with its stale air and out into fresh air that can invigorate you.

Some short exercises in both breathing and stretching also can be very beneficial during the work day to improve concentration. Such exercises are described in more detail in chapter eleven.

Dr. Benjamin Spock, when asked by the author if he has any special techniques for concentration, responded briefly:

"Never solved the problem of concentration!"

John Train, a highly successful Wall Street financial advisor, replied to the same question:

"Sorry! No special techniques except being interested in what I'm doing."

Interest — the key to better concentration, as many other successful men and women say over and over again.

Linda P. Gallagher, executive director of the Alliance to Save Energy, Washington, D.C., responded to my request for techniques to aid concentration in greater depth:

"I have found a couple of factors I find to be most important in my ability to concentrate. First, I must make a conscious decision about what to focus in on, and then reserve a set amount of time for that particular subject, without interruption. To help me make that basic decision, I make lists and prioritize my projects. The commitment to see a particular problem through to its resolution is my prime motivator.

"The next step is to reserve a certain amount of time to work on the issue and to minimize interruption. I very consciously choose the period for concentration based on such factors as time of day and physical environment, and correlate these to what I perceive to be the difficulty of the problem.

"If the problem is terribly difficult and requires absolute quiet and concentration, I isolate myself in my home environment. On a difficult issue, I will simply have my phone calls held and shut my office door. As a normal day-to-day routine, I work with my door open and take calls as they come in, easily returning to work on my desk.

"Whereas some people are not bothered by noise, I find that my concentration is impaired by having the radio on, etc. For me, a quiet environment enhances concentration."

Eustace Miles, who wrote on concentration in business some years ago, says that the best managers of businesses can themselves perform each part of the business consciously. They train each employee to perform his proper function. They prefer, afterwards, to delegate the details to these employees, and to themselves direct the whole, only occasionally supervising the details.

So it should also be with concentration. We should be training ourselves in each part of our work, so that the conscious self can perform every part well. Then we can delegate the work to the special under-mind which regulates it, so that the conscious self may be devoted to the most important matters of management — or to play or rest. Concentration cannot succeed without businesslike methods, says Miles.

If we are interested in a task, it is no trouble to concentrate on it. We can't do anything else. Consequently, if we want to concentrate on a particular subject, we must *get interested* in it.

In work, if our dominant interest is not in harmony with our business, the business will suffer. If we concentrate continually on trivial incidents of life while we should be concentrating on our work — if we "butterfly around," as Thomas Edison put it — we will be "useless woolgatherers."

Alexander Graham Bell once remarked, "Concentrate all your thoughts upon the work in hand. The sun's rays do not burn until brought to a focus."

If you can't sustain concentration at work for very long periods, try the approach taken by Edward Henry Harriman, the great railroad builder. He said that his decisions, which were often monumental, were the product of brief periods of intense application in which he reviewed all the conditions and elements involved and forged his conclusions, as it were, at white heat.

Working at an uninteresting task will tend to make it interesting. The more you work at any job and the more you know about it, the easier it will be for you to concentrate on it.

Focus your interest on a specific thing. You can't concentrate on any big, vague subject, nor on several things at once.

Begin the habit of being interested in a small way. Select something simple, devote a short time to it at first, and select a time and place where there are few disturbing influences.

Do not consciously try to concentrate. *Get interested*, and concentration will take care of itself, so that you can work toward achieving the flow that makes work more satisfying, even if it may never really be "fun."

6
Concentration
in Sport and Leisure

Most of us can learn lessons in concentration from athletes. Maybe their concentration is so keen on their particular game or sport because they are so interested in it. They love what they're doing.

Athletes often can achieve a seemingly effortless concentration even under the greatest pressures of competition, and with thousands of people watching their every move. Golfers, tennis pros, distance runners, and other sportsmen and sportswomen often can achieve a "flow" (which we discussed in chapter five) that seems to transport them out of their minds and bodies. They become one with their golf clubs or tennis rackets or running shoes.

Swimmers, basketball and baseball players, even rock climbers have described the experience of flow they get out of their sport. "You're so involved in what you're doing, you aren't thinking of yourself as separate from the immediate activity," one rock climber has explained. Another added, "It is not moving up but a continuous flowing; you move up only to keep the flow going. There is no possible reason for the climbing except the climbing itself. It is a self-communication."

William Barry Furlong, who has written on many

subjects including the psychological aspects of athletics, says that athletes he has talked to about their experiences flowing tell him that "your body feels good and awake all over. Your energy is flowing . . ."

But not everyone who takes up a sport or leisure activity can achieve flow.

No matter if not all of us are fortunate enough to achieve flow in sports or recreation. We can all benefit from the discipline we learn from the concentration needed to play a good game of tennis, golf, or even from jogging.

In many games, the successful player keeps his eye on the ball. This is noticeably the case in golf, handball, tennis, and other sports involving an object to be struck or caught. But the successful athlete also will keep part of his attention on what else is going on around him as he plays the game.

Some people feel they are too busy to take up a sport, or they think games are a waste of time which could be spent on more serious things, like more work. But carrying any business or study in the mind all the time, day and night, morning and evening, does not really advance that business so well as does forgetting it at intervals and letting the mind rest, just as you allow your muscles to rest after any physical exertion. The mind allowed to rest gains new ideas and new force to carry out ideas.

One researcher into concentration suggests that the remedy for better concentration is to have more recreation, more variety of occupation. More selves in our one self. To attain the highest and happiest life we need to combine two (or even more) lives in one — to be merchant in the morning, and artist or yachtsman or handball player in the afternoon. In the second life we should forget for the time all about the first. We can rest the first life or set of faculties, recuperate them, refresh them, and go back to business, or art or science, or any occupation, next day with more force, plan, idea, thought to put into it. Apart from the practice of concentration, which can be very easy when we engage in a sport or a recreation such as gardening, these activities provide a rest for the mind so that it can come back to its work with fresh power of concentration.

Many athletes are fortunate enough to feel that their work is also their recreation. Some people enjoy their work so much that they don't think they need recreation or a vacation. But most of us can benefit from participating in a sport or recreation, not only to help refresh our minds and bodies, but to learn techniques of concentration we gain from such activity.

We can learn a great deal about improving our attention from athletics. Sports often help us develop our skills in improving the direction of our attention — broadening or narrowing it, for example.

A baseball pitcher can develop an internal focus in order to decide how to pitch to a left-handed batter. Then he shifts his attention to external stimuli, such as the catcher's mitt, in order to pitch. If strategy changes after he throws the pitch, the ballplayer then goes back to an internal focus.

As a general rule, according to Robert Nideffer in his study, *The Inner Athlete*, the more complex and rapidly changing the situation, the more externally focused your attention must be. And conversely, as the need for analysis or planning increases, the more internal and reflective your focus becomes.

Sports also help us to *visualize*, another technique beneficial to concentration. A basketball player about to shoot a free throw will bounce the ball in front of himself several times and look up at the basket to visualize himself sinking a shot. Likewise, a golfer will concentrate on visualizing the path his ball will take on the green as he prepares to sink a crucial putt.

Sportsmen often are able to anticipate the moves of their opponents, to predict in advance what their competition will do next. Like chess players, they can visualize their opponents' moves before they make them, to gain the advantage.

Many sportspersons say they don't know *how* they concentrate. Bruce Jenner, the Olympic decathlon winner, is typical of athletes who attribute their success to practice or training. But they *do* concentrate when they practice; they just may not be aware of *how* they concentrate. We can take lessons from the many athletes who share with us in this chapter their thoughts on how they concentrate.

Marty Liquori, one of America's greatest runners of 1,000 and 5,000 meter races, tells how he concentrates before and during an event:

"About forty-five minutes or an hour before a race, I just block out all other thoughts. I don't allow any outside influences to even enter my mind, once I start my warm-up jogging. The mental part of me also has to turn on, so that even if someone was to say hello to me then, I probably wouldn't even answer. If the track fell apart as I was warming up on one end, I just wouldn't let it enter my mind. I think you can do that in any activity. You can tell your mind 'Don't deal with that distraction. Stay on the one track and think about the race.'

"I think about the possible scenarios that might develop as the race goes on, and how I'm going to respond to them. It's just a matter of concentrating on anything that could happen during the race, and nothing else in the world.

"When many people have a big event to point for, whether it's in sport or business or whatever, they make the mistake of trying to get excited and concentrate on it for days before the event. But by the time they come to it, their mental energies and their adrenalin are worn down. During the final hour or two before the event, they may let some little thing like someone saying hello right before the race break their concentration.

"I use this technique when I'm preparing for a speech. It doesn't do me much good if I concentrate on the thoughts I'm going to use in the speech four days in advance of giving it. But the last two hours before it, I try to lock myself in a room and just think about the speech. Then I'm really up for it.

Concentration *in* a race is a little different. Runners fall into two categories. One is a runner who *disassociates* while he runs. He tries to think about something else and not about the pain his body might be going through. But that type of person is really a jogger. Anyone who is competitive and wants to win a race has to *associate* when they run. They're thinking constantly about the weather and track conditions or the signals they're getting from their body, such as 'Am I using my arms too much?' or 'Are my legs getting tired?' or 'Was the early pace too fast?'

"Those who associate during a race are looking inward at themselves. In a race of only a few minutes, if a runner dissociates for even a minute, he can all of a sudden be left twenty yards behind, because he loses contact with the leader. In running, contact is always a big thing; not to lose contact with leaders in front.

"So you're concentrating on your body — your form. The strengths you know the other guy may have, and the weaknesses you might have. There may be 18,000 people screaming around you, but you are perhaps totally concentrating on the shoulder muscles of the runner in front of you. You might notice the most slight tightening of his shoulder muscles, which might give you an indication that he's getting tired and now is the time to pass him.

"Again, you're trying to concentrate on one thing at a time, and rule out all outside influences that don't have any real bearing on the task at hand. This is probably also true of golfers and tennis players, who are tremendous at concentrating on the ball."

Liquori says he likens running to the mental discipline of a yogi or someone who can go into a trance:

"After years of racing, once the gun goes off you know what to expect and you can get into a certain frame of mind which may be similar to what many people go through when they are in meditation. It takes years of practice, but it's only successful if you are totally committed to it.

"There were races where I was prepared to hurt, or to do certain things no matter how bad I felt when I got out there or what the competition was doing. I had a total commitment to run until I dropped. That doesn't really happen in an hour before the race. It's the sum of months of training, confidence from that training, and a lot of upbringing in your formative years. To me, concentration and commitment go hand in hand. In anything, such as in giving a speech, if you're not committed, you can't concentrate."

Tom Fleming, who has run more sub-2:20 marathons than perhaps any other American, twice winner of the New York Marathon and twice second-place finisher of the Boston Marathon, says that sometimes it's good to be able to both keep your mind on what you are doing and to take your mind off of it.

"But when you're really into whatever you're doing," says Fleming, "you have to be able to concentrate totally. So if there's any advantage, I'd rather be a person who can get really into whatever I'm doing. In my case, it's training 20 miles a day, 140 miles a week. When I'm running, whether it's for training or in competition, I have to put my mind to it.

"I think a lot of it has to do with being positive in your thoughts. I always correlate concentration with positive thinking. A lot of athletes do the same. During a race, when you're really concentrating hard, time passes by very quickly. During training runs, I may want to concentrate hard because it makes the time pass. I'm not saying that running is boring, but you do have your times when it seems tedious.

"While training in a really hard workout, I try to

keep my concentration on exactly what I'm doing. I'm evaluating the physical aspects of my body. At other times, I can be running and think about just about anything. When I was in college, I used to do a lot of my hard thinking on problems. Now that I own a running store, while I'm running I think about how I can improve myself as a businessperson or how I can run my business better.

"But at times, you have to have the ability to totally concentrate on what you're doing. In a race situation, you have to be constantly aware of everything around you, so during a competition, my mind will be totally on my running and the race. If you're highly motivated, I believe your ability to concentrate can help you win races. Desire is very important. Once you lose it, or lose your ability to concentrate, you're through."

Concentration is considered by many tennis pros to be the secret to their game. Some of them have learned how to concentrate by following the advice of the famous tennis coach Pop Fuller to Rod Laver, Helen Wills, and Helen Jacobs. He suggests that every time the ball hits the court, you should say "bounce" to yourself. Every time you or your opponent hit the ball, say "hit." Be sure to say it at exactly the same time that the ball bounces or the ball is hit. This takes total concentration and all nervousness or other distractions will disappear.

Ethan Gologor, psychologist at the City University of New York, has written that tennis is a dynamic; things are constantly changing — not only who is about to hit the ball and from what side of the court you're about to serve, but what your opponent is thinking and what you think about what he's thinking. The more you are aware of in tennis, the better you can defend yourself. The same, he maintains, is true of life.

Gologor also suggests that much of the play in tennis, and your ability to concentrate on it, depends on the *sounds* of the game as well as the *sights*. In tennis you react as much to the sound of the racket meeting the ball as to the sight of the ball in play. Therefore, concentration in tennis is intertwined with either silence or a constant, muted sound pattern.

Temperament also comes into play in tennis concentration. For some superstars, such as Jimmy Connors, concentration is not broken and apparently is enhanced by "cutting up" on the court — talking to the spectators, performing little hip-dances when narrowly making a point, or sometimes even wagging a finger at an opponent, playing the extrovert. Bjorn Borg, the quintessential introvert, rarely shows any emotion beyond an occasional curling of the lip when he double-faults.

Gologor maintains that if the introvert can hang in there at the beginning of a match, he will win. If the extrovert does not build up an early lead, he will lose.

Bjorn Borg, master of the sport which demands the utmost individual concentration, is so unflappable on the court, so able to block out the crowd noise that can distract him and affect his play, he has earned from his opponents the nickname "The Iceborg." In a sport which is truly a contest of wills, this ability to completely control his emotions has indeed aided Borg in his single-minded determination to achieve his overriding goal — to win tennis tournaments.

Vince Eldred, the tennis pro and teacher, says not to concentrate on the direction of the ball in play. A split-second look can cause a poor shot. Your objective in tennis is to keep the opponent moving by hitting the ball away from him. The direction, angle, and depth of your preceding shot should tell you where your opponent is going to be after his return.

Regardless of what tennis players call it, says Eldred, whether it's psyching themselves for a match, building self-motivation, achieving mental toughness, or whatever they call the "it" they need to win, it all adds up to concentration. All else are words or phrases "irrevocably interwoven with a players ability to maintain and sustain long periods of intense concentration."

Eldred suggests following the belief of Dr. Maxwell Maltz, author of *Psycho-Cybernetics*, that as a concentration tool in tennis it is best to use your imagination to visualize yourself in action. Think your shot through, from inception to conclusion. Picture to yourself just how you would act if you had already succeeded with an action.

Part of concentration, says Eldred, is the ability to perceive and adjust your game when it becomes necessary.

Billie Jean King says concentration is one of the primary strengths of her game. She doesn't watch her opponent or anything else but concentrates on the ball, especially from the time it leaves her opponent's racket to the time she hits it with hers.

Jim Brown, physical education authority, says the key to concentration in tennis is to block out as much as you can from your mind, leaving only the game to think about. But since a match can last from one to three hours and it may be impossible to sustain total concentration that long, the goal becomes one of mentally eliminating as many distractions as possible while you are on the court. Ignore the crowds watching or the players in the courts next to you. Play your own match. When play begins, don't worry about how good your opponent may be. Play the best game you can, and play *your* game, not his or hers.

If you can't control noise while playing tennis, try to learn to accept it. If you can play well and concentrate when it's noisy around the court, you will be able to concentrate even better when it's quiet.

Don't allow your mind to wander. Keep your thoughts on the game, playing one point at a time. Avoid unnecessary talking. Don't give up after making a bad shot; concentrate on making the next one better. Become as totally absorbed in the match as you possibly can. Make each point the most important thing in your life and you will be able to keep your mind on your game.

Handball is a game that is decided by inches of difference between you and your opponent. Paul Haber, former national singles handball champion and author of *Inside Handball*, says anticipation is one means of gaining precious inches for yourself, and that concentration is another. Haber trained himself to sense his opponent's tenseness at particular points in the game. He could read the other player's frame of mind the way a good poker player reads mental sets at the gaming table.

Handball is the kind of sport that forces you to concentrate on what is happening now if you expect to stay in the game, says Haber. If your mind wanders onto personal or business or other problems, "you're quickly a pigeon on that court." Handball requires a mental approach of "forced, determined calm and concentration."

"I like to think of waiting for an opponent's serve as just as mind-clearing as the yoga technique of imagining yourself in a long, dark tunnel concentrating on a lit candle at the far end of the tunnel. If you are concentrating properly on a handball court, the only job you have in the world is to return that little black ball in such a way and to such a point that your opponent will not be able to return it to you."

Haber says a friend who is a psychiatrist credits his handball playing with keeping *him* off the couch. It helps him get rid of his aggressions and frustrations without naming them. But he focuses his attention totally on the game. He's thinking about returning that little black ball where his opponent can't get to it.

Arnold Palmer says there are four essentials involved in playing a better game of golf, quite apart from the way a person handles his clubs. Palmer, in *Situation Golf*, calls them the "Four C's": concentration, confidence, competitive urge, and capacity for enjoyment.

"All of these qualities are interrelated," says Palmer. "The reason I put concentration at the top of the list is because I have never known a great performer—and over the years I have known champions in many sports—who didn't have the ability to concentrate completely. What do I mean by concentration? I mean focusing totally on the business at hand and commanding your body to do exactly what you want it to do.

"When my father, the finest golf teacher I have ever known, began to train me to play the game, the first thing he taught me was to concentrate. Day in and day out he would drum into me the need to fix my mind on every part of the game. He taught me not to fool around.

"Never allow yourself to get into the habit of taking the game too lightly or you'll make a farce of it. If you've just missed a second putt, don't poke at the ball just because it's only a foot from the pin.

"Develop certain habits that go with concentration. Before you stand up to a ball at the tee, for example, step back and survey the layout from tee to green. Know every curve in the fairway and where the rough suddenly widens and the fairway narrows. Know how far it is from the tee to the middle-distance traps or other hazards, and the best area to hit your approach shot. Know where the danger areas are on the green so that your approach doesn't bounce into a trap or skid down an embankment.

"In short, even before you step up to the ball, have a full battle plan for the hole worked out."

Palmer says the problem many golfers have with their games is not so much a matter of technique as of strategy:

"If we learn to concentrate on our golf game, we can develop the strategy needed to shave strokes off our game."

Dai Reese, champion British golfer and golf teacher, has said that to be a successful golfer one must close the mind to the extent that the stroke which is being played is the only thing that matters.

A psychiatrist and golf writer, Dr. David C. Morley, says that we can develop our ability to concentrate on our game, whether it is golf or any other sport. We must concentrate on every stroke and not allow "tension to leak into our nervous system." Concentration in golf should lead us to action, not to Transcendental Meditation. Good golfers don't play in a trance, they play with active minds that are aware of every aspect of the game.

Many athletes "take a breather" before attempting to score a crucial point, as golfers may do before trying to sink a winning putt. Perhaps unknowingly, when we take a breather in sport we are borrowing from the Eastern meditative disciplines. A few deep breaths of air before attempting a crucial point in sports can help relax us and also focus our attention on what we are attempting. High-divers take a deep breath before going off the diving board. Basketball players do it before shooting from the foul line. Baseball pitchers do it before winding up for a pitch.

Try it the next time you are in a tight spot in your sport. When the pressure is on, pause for a moment, close your eyes, and take a couple of deep breaths of air before you attempt to master the crucial situation.

In baseball, coaches Ray Merkle and Bobby Shantz maintain that the attitude of *patient concentration* is the most important single characteristic of a good hitter. This frame of mind is what makes all the rest jell.

The batter should try to observe the catcher's pattern of calls to the pitcher. This can help him to guess the next pitch. He should also watch closely how the infielders and outfielders station themselves. Their positioning might be giveaways to the pitcher's strategy. A batter must focus on what he is doing while remaining aware of what else is going on around him. Other players may be sending messages to each other which he can turn to his own benefit.

Once you develop good habits of concentration in any sport, your game begins to "work" for you. You appear to play well almost effortlessly and automatically.

Janet Guthrie, probably the world's leading woman race car driver, shares her thoughts on concentration with us:

"Unfortunately, I can't tell you exactly how I've gained the concentration necessary to race. It is certainly the most important single thing, as I've pointed out many times, and back some eighteen years ago I did have to work hard at it. Now, it comes naturally; but I don't know exactly how."

The answer to how many top athletes concentrate is a combination of interest, determination, and the desire to be best. Focusing all their attention on the moment at hand, blocking out all distractions, they are able to tune out the rest of the world around them and sink the putt, belt the home run, or break the finish-line tape. Once they condition themselves to concentrate on what they are doing, they achieve the "flow" that makes it all look so easy and effortless to us onlookers.

Jon Erickson of Chicago, a young friend of mine and one of the top marathon swimmers in the world, a few years ago broke all records by swimming the English Channel both ways, a total distance of forty-two bone-chilling miles. He broke the standing world record which had been set by his own father ten years before. Jon swam the round-trip in thirty hours flat, beating his father's record by only three minutes.

"Distance swimming is like living a small lifetime," Jon says. "You get your ups and downs in swimming something like the English Channel, just as you do in living your life. You have to concentrate on how to win over the challenge ahead of you. You have to face the challenges and keep fighting the obstacles. There's no other way to do it.

"After ten hours in the water, I lost the strength and determination I had started with. But I was getting close to the French coast then, and when I asked myself why I was torturing my body and mind this way, I knew the answer. I wanted this challenge. I wanted to prove to myself that I could do it. And I just made up my mind to keep going.

"Two hours later I reached the French coast and got a ten-minute rest. Swimming from France back to England in the dark was strange and eerie. But it was also beautiful, seeing the lights from ships making the crossing. And each time I extended my arm for another stroke, the water bubbled in a beautiful phosphorescent glow.

"I hummed to myself as I swam. I have a great built-in radio inside me. I hummed Beatles songs and took my mind off of the swim by thinking about my girl-friend. I reminded myself how much my folks and my girlfriend were rooting for me.

"Covering the last two miles to the English shore

should have taken me only an hour, but instead it took five hours because of the current. It was then that I had to force myself to make the swim a case of mind over matter. My Dad had taught me that you can do that with any challenge, and now I had to see if I could make his philosophy work for me.

"I found that I *could* find the energy . . . that I *could* find the determination to keep on going. I learned that your mind can amaze your body, if you just keep telling yourself, *I can do it . . . I can do it . . . I can do it!*

"Marathon swimming has taught me to accept the things in life that are hard to accept. It's a mental discipline that you learn."

Writing in *The Silent Pulse,* a study of "the search for the perfect rhythm that exists in each of us," George Leonard reports that athletes in every field from golf to weightlifting are unequivocal in stating that "mental" or "psychological" factors are primary in achieving top performance. "Technical measures are involved in building the base camp," says Leonard. "But the journey from there to the peak is all intentionality."

Leonard quotes Arnold Schwarzenegger, five times Mr. Universe and the world's premier body-builder, as stating, "The mind is the limit. As long as the mind can envision the fact that you can do something, you can do it—as long as you really believe 100 percent. It's all mind over matter."

Using the concentration technique of visualization, Leonard reports, Schwarzenegger *thinks* his way into a certain muscle and visualizes it as larger. He lifts weights mentally before doing it physically.

113

"The first step," says Schwarzenegger, "is to create the vision, because when you see the vision there—the beautiful vision—that creates the 'want power.'"

Leonard describes a state of consciousness in which the athlete achieves "focused surrender," when "intentionality has a powerful influence on the world of matter." He suggests exercises by which the athlete can achieve the experience of perfect rhythm which involves intense concentration on breathing and body maneuvers.

In San Francisco, James L. Hickman of The Transformation Project is leading research into how the body and mind are transformed in different disciplines such sports, dance, the martial arts, etc. The project is designed to elaborate the variety of unexplored human potentials which are accessible, to discover the ways in which such capacities manifest themselves and to develop psycho-physical techniques which facilitate them.

Hickman points out that for some years now, Soviet researchers have been combining techniques from meditation, yoga, hypnosis, autogenic training, and the martial arts to form a "Psychical Self-Regulation" training system for their athletes. Through extensive laboratory research they learned that most people, without physiological feedback, could quickly learn to control their heart rates, blood circulation, pain threshhold, and muscle tension through a combination of internal processes. The purpose of PSR training is to develop a person's natural ability to influence his or her own physiological functions by purposefully directed mental processes.

While much of super-success in sports can be attributed to the old saw of "mind over matter," more is being learned now about just how that happens. This can benefit not only those who aspire to become tomorrow's Arnold Palmers and Arnold Schwarzeneggers, but also the rest of us who just want to play a good game, jog a good few miles, and reap the rewards physically, emotionally, and intellectually.

7

The Roles of
Mood and Environment
in Concentration

Louis Lamour, whose western novels have sold better than those of any other writer in history, says he could concentrate on his writing while squatting Indian-style with his typewriter at the intersection of Hollywood and Vine.

John Steinbeck had to write his novels in private with no distractions—that included wife and children.

Adlai Stevenson says his father, the late senator, could achieve high levels of concentration even in the most adverse circumstances. "I believe it was because of an abundance of interest and enthusiasm for whatever he was doing," Stevenson recalls.

Hugh Downs, the popular and very busy television personality has a four-step technique for concentration:

"I know there are times when I'm highly motivated and able to concentrate with some fierceness of focus, but most of the time I enjoy the fuzziness of a mental myopia that provides a vast mulch from which my abilities and my reputation as a generalist no doubt arise. (A generalist you remember is a person who comes to know less and less about more and more until he knows practically nothing about everything.)

"It does appear to have to do with motivation, and my serious thoughts on the matter are that to concentrate on anything requires a sincerity of interest and some ongoing effort to exclude the normal extraneous impulses that bombard us all of our waking hours. This involves some combination of:

1) Removing oneself to a quiet place.
2) Picking hours when phones are unlikely to ring.
3) Informing acquaintances and loved ones of a desire not to be disturbed (and)
4) Logging triumphs in sustained concentration, so that a sense of accomplishment will add itself to the initial motivation."

The mood we are in, whether positive or depressed, and the environment we work or study in often play major roles in our ability to concentrate.

Time of day affects some people's powers of concentration. Early morning best suits most people who have tried concentrating at various times of day, while others find evening the best time. Some cannot concentrate during a full moon which, we know, often plays funny tricks on the mind. A few exceptional people can manage to concentrate best in the early afternoon.

Some people can concentrate on work they bring along on an airplane, while others cannot concentrate in planes but can get work done on train trips.

Muscular tension helps many people to concentrate better at first, but then afterwards they are helped more by muscular relaxation.

The writer Arthur Koestler has said that his best writing mood comes when obstacles are eliminated from his mind. These might include worries about whether the drains function in his home or whether the reviews for his latest book are good or bad.

Koestler believes that depression and elation are both conducive to creativity, but most important is not to be deflected or obsessed with anything outside the work. He finds concentration to be an eliminatory process of his defenses against extraneous matter.

The popular playwright Neil Simon has different views on mood, concentration, and productivity. One of the most prolific of writers, Simon admits he can turn on his creative powers of concentration almost at will, like plugging in an electric typewriter. Sometimes he can't think of anything to write until he sits down at his typewriter, but then the minute he does, his creativity begins and concentration follows. He says he can work almost anywhere, if he has to.

The composer Aaron Copland says he needs ideal conditions for concentration. He has to be in his studio, where conditions are conducive to work and where he will not have any distractions. If he feels in the mood to write, something starts him off. He might feel sad, he might feel lonely. He might feel elated. He might have gotten a good letter from a friend. Something starts him off and he is productive.

Copland admits to being a night worker. He knows many other composers who work best very early in the morning when their minds are clear and they feel **fresh and rested. But by 10 A.M. they are not able to work anymore.**

Bonnie Cashin, the fashion designer, says that if she is physically uncomfortable, working in a small, cramped, disorderly space, she feels tired and irritable and cannot be creative or productive. Her thoughts

119

are slowed down. If she feels that the refinement of an idea to its best potential is at the mercy of elements beyond her control, frustration sets in and she becomes discouraged. But the situation reversed can spark great concentration and productivity.

Ms. Cashin says that sometimes intense emotional happenings have had the effect of intensifying creative action for her. It may be the weather. She likes sunshine, and oppressive weather depresses her. If her body feels good, and the environment is attractive or interesting, she is likely to be content and can screen out most disruptions of a day so she can concentrate and be productive.

The movie director Sidney Lumet says tension destroys his concentration and creativity. When anything starts to go wrong or any unhappiness enters his day or night, he stops work and contemplates the tension that has arisen, to get it right out in the open and deal with it. Only coming to grips with the cause of the tension releases him so he can get back to work.

Many people believe that physical condition is paramount in allowing them to concentrate well. Feeling either rested or tired may have a great effect on their work.

The novelist Isaac Bashevis Singer has said that being depressed and being happy are so near to one another that sometimes he doesn't know the difference. He finds that it can be one little step that makes the difference between happiness and depression. But being very depressed, experiencing a real crisis of despair, is not conducive to one's work.

On the other hand, the noted astronomer Harlow

Shapley says he works better when he is depressed. If he has difficulty concentrating on a project, he does not drop it and pick it up again later. He sticks with it right to the limit of his ability, until he has conquered it.

Alma Boice Holland, prolific writer of stories and articles for many popular magazines, has observed that more and more it is becoming difficult to be alone and that this is a basic need for all people—the need for solitude. Life is crowded, it moves quickly, but it is often necessary to shut it out.

A quiet period in the day refreshes mental powers and helps us to diminish the clutter of daily cares. Ms. Holland believes the writer has to withdraw from intimate associations occasionally to make space for reflection and time for private thinking. She reminds us that the psalmist David produced his loveliest songs in solitude.

But silence also has an invigorating and restorative effect, producing a quiet rhythm essential for writing and concentration. Opportunities to be alone and undisturbed must be created. They will not come of themselves and modern life is certainly not soundproof.

Since concentration is the act of focusing attention upon the job at hand, distractions foreign to the present project must be eliminated. This can come naturally if the writer is intensely interested in his material. Delaying tactics such as sharpening pencils, cleaning the typewriter keyboard, or fixing a snack only delays operation-concentration.

Ms. Holland believes setting a goal will help toward greater concentration, because it stimulates the mental

121

energies to meet it and offers the incentive to succeed. Short-term goals are best because they are more manageable.

Dr. Joyce Brothers has similar thoughts:

"I promise myself a reward upon the successful completion of a task I set myself. The reward is a small one—an apple, a walk, a phone call I want to make, etc.

"This way, I use possible distractions as incentives."

A technique valuable in helping the mind concentrate on the matter of the moment is to jot down ideas. Write out key thoughts as they come to consciousness and they will keep you in the mood for creative thinking. They also tend to bring forth a train of associated information which has been stored away in your memory.

Since the brain works at high speed, it must be regulated to stay on the track and prevented from taking excursions into unrelated fields of thought. Realization that the average mind does tend to wander makes it necessary to maintain a high level of interest in the work at hand, and to exercise self-discipline. This is not easy, but it can be done.

Concentration and creativity often come to us in strange ways. Samuel Johnson needed to have a purring cat around, along with orange peel and plenty of tea to drink. Balzac wrote all night, stimulated by constant cups of strong black coffee. Emile Zola pulled down the blinds at midday because he found more stimulus for his thought in artificial light. On the other hand, today we learn that artificial light can be harmful to us, both visually and creatively.

Many people work hard at trying to create a soundproof environment in which to concentrate. The problem is not new. Thomas Carlyle was forever trying to construct a soundproof room to write in, while Marcel Proust is said to have actually achieved one.

Friedrich Schiller, the German poet and dramatist, depended on the smell of decomposing apples to help him concentrate on his writing. He kept them concealed in his writing desk.

Rudyard Kipling could not create with a lead pencil. His thought processes demanded the blackest ink, all bluish-blacks being "an abomination" to his creative genius.

Not that they are comparable in creativity, but the late French philosopher Rene Descartes and the American publisher Hugh Hefner have at least one thing in common. Descartes spent his early life in an environment which permitted him to indulge his wish—or perhaps it was his intellectual necessity—to work in bed. Hefner became famous for editing his magazine from his satin-sheeted oval bed in the Playboy mansion in Chicago, while lounging in bold silk pajamas, the proverbial pipe in mouth.

The philosopher Immanuel Kant also did some of his best thinking in bed, but at certain precise times of day. His blankets had to be mounded up around him in a special way. For security? Only Charlie Brown's friend Linus may know for sure.

Some trees grew up outside Kant's window and obscured a tower on which he had mentally focused when thinking out his famous essay, *Critique of Pure Reason.* It is doubtful the work would have been completed if

123

the trees had not been ordered cut down. The book is both one of the most difficult and one of the most important achievements of philosophical thinking, and Kant's rigid requirements about his surroundings were perhaps essential to the level of intellectual functioning and endurance that were needed to produce it.

Sigmund Freud chain-smoked while he worked out what was substantially a new branch of science. During periods of national crisis, his friends and associates were careful to make sure he had a good supply of cheroots.

Some people work best in familiar surroundings, while others concentrate better in new environments. Working in a familiar place involves subjecting yourself to a vast number of subliminal sensory cues which have become associatively linked with work activity.

The act of working in a place one finds congenial for work provides for a sensory input of cues that have in the past provoked thought or concentration, sustained endurance, and perhaps been fruitful in evoking original ideas. The effect of such stimuli cannot be ignored, particularly in any explanation of *sustained* creative thinking.

Emotion, feeling, mood, and temperament are obviously important components of concentration and creativity.

Neighborhood noises drove me to move my office from my dining room to my basement two winters ago. It was one of the smartest moves I ever made.

I paneled a large storage room, piled books high up against the noisiest side of the room for insulation (from my neighbors' barking dogs), moved all my file cabinets and reference books down around me and began to concentrate on my work better than I ever imagined I could.

The room is about as soundproof as it can be made, and my productivity has increased tremendously because I have reduced or eliminated many distracting neighborhood and household noises. Soft music I play on two stereo speakers in my office, hooked up to the living room sound equipment, drowns out most of the rest of the environmental noises.

The trick is to find a room in your house or apartment where you can concentrate best on whatever work you have to do. A friend converted part of his attic to a workroom similar to my basement office. In the evenings when he works at home, he and his wife arrange that their two children play in their own playroom in the basement so the sounds do not carry upstairs to the attic.

A young housewife across the street, mother of four youngsters, is also a professional artist. She and her husband had part of their basement made into a studio where she paints after putting the children to bed. Many times she burns the post-midnight oil until two or three A.M., happily concentrating on her painting without any of the distractions of her life as a mother during the daylight hours. Any loss of sleep is, she feels, worth it, to be creative and recharge her emotional batteries.

Music often can help us shut out external noises and increase our ability to concentrate. However, young people who think they can study while listening to rock music on the radio or phonograph are kidding themselves, according to recent research. The unusual beat that is characteristic of rock music can interfere with normal brain wave activity and cause a dip in strength.

This "stopped anapestic" beat is just the opposite of the heartbeat and pulse and may act as a stress signal that disrupts the alpha waves normally flowing between the two hemispheres of the brain. When this happens, the regular brain signals to the muscles may become disrupted and cause weakness.

A friend's teenage daughter just wrote me saying a typical rock concert is about two hours of noise that may permanently damage her ears, "but it's heavenly!"

Dr. Denton A. Cooley, a cardiovascular specialist with the Texas Heart Institute in Houston, tells how music can help him both relax and concentrate better:

"While some people seem to be able to concentrate in the presence of extraneous noise, this is quite distracting for me. I am unable to listen to certain types of music while I am trying to concentrate. While silence is my preferred atmosphere, I can concentrate with softly-played classical, not contemporary music.

"My best concentration is done at a desk with a straight chair or a swivel chair. I am unable to concentrate seriously while sitting or lying in bed. My best hours of concentration are late at night or early in the morning. These are the quiet periods in my life."

Several phonograph recordings are now available which are made especially to help us relax and to improve our powers of concentration.

One such record, *Programming for Better Concentration*, reportedly can help the listener attain the automatically correct results of an electronic computer. The subconscious mind, having been programmed to react automatically to intellectual stimuli, furnishes the correct response pattern whenever such stimuli are encountered. It is basically the same method mathematicians and scientists or other problem-solvers use. It is available from the Wilshire Book Company, 8721 Sunset Boulevard, Hollywood, California 90069.

An entire series of records with music and other sounds conducive to relaxation and concentration are produced by Syntonic Research, Inc., Atlantic Recording Corporation, 1841 Broadway, New York, New York 10023. Called *Environments,* the recordings also are available at many record shops.

Environments recordings are designed to be "heard," rather than "listened to." The brain hears the sounds with both ears simultaneously, and since they are pleasant, familiar sounds, attention, concentration, and relaxation potentials increase.

Two discs in the series are especially designed as thought enhancers—*The Psychologically Ultimate Ocean* and *Tintinnabulation.* The ocean record contains restful sounds of waves splashing against the shore. The other record contains the sound of bells, but bells so dulcet and beautiful that they affect the subconscious in totally unexpected ways. Five different bells, each sounded very softly, reverberating for minutes afterward, produce sounds which seem to float in the air, moving around the room you are listening in as a physical presence. Both recordings are highly useful for meditation, concentration, and relaxation.

Other recordings in the *Environments* series also help shut out distracting noises and help the listener to relax, study, or concentrate better. *Summer Cornfield* is a tapestry of natural sounds—a sea of summer insects, from the complex hiss of katydids to the chirp of meadow grasshoppers and the drone of cicadas.

Intonation is a recording of massed voices blending over an extraordinary range to create harmonics and undertones which have been compared to sustained chords on the middle register of an enormous pipe organ. The basic flow carries you along with the voices, and it is often both easy and pleasant to join in with your own voice, which can aid your concentration.

A recording perfectly suited for noise cancellation is *Gentle Rain in a Pine Forest*, a psychoacoustic effect with sounds of insects and distant birds. The primary sound is that of summer rain gently dripping upon pine needles. It masks most low level noises as the sound represents, from a psychological point of view, the quietude of a pine forest.

Some years ago, Cole Porter wrote a beautiful ballad called "I Concentrate on You." It really works. When you hear a favorite song played or sung, one that you associate with a person or event important in your life, it tends to bring that person or event vividly into your mind. If you are lonely or troubled, sad or depressed, or feeling that your nerves are at the breaking point, think of a person you love or a favorite place such as a garden or seashore. Concentrating on the person or place, or on an activity such as paddling a canoe on a tranquil lake, helps you to relax and change your mood.

128

When we hear a classical violinist such as Isaac Stern we are amazed at his powers of concentration. While playing the violin, he is totally absorbed in his music and his concentration is almost beyond belief to us. We wish we could learn how to concentrate that well, but perhaps we give up and attribute his concentration to the fact that he is a genius.

But William James, the father of modern psychology, said that geniuses differ from ordinary people not in any innate quality of the brain, but merely in regard to the subjects and purposes upon which they concentrate, and in the degree of concentration which they manage to achieve.

Modern educational experiments tend to prove James was right. Any normal child or adult can be taught to concentrate 100 percent of his faculties upon a given task or problem, and be certain that he will produce astonishing results.

The capacity for concentration is in no sense the exclusive property of genius. Aldous Huxley said that every child is a genius until the age of ten. Was there ever greater absorption than a child can show when he is deep in a book or engrossed with a new toy or game? Children can give concentration in its purest form to matters important to them.

Concentration has been called "interest in action." It is not an unnatural state that goes contrary to our normal way of functioning. Unless you permit yourself to become absorbed like a child, or an absent-minded professor so wrapped up in his favorite subject he doesn't know it's raining outside, there is very little chance that you will do your thing well enough

129

to produce results that are truly outstanding, whether it be playing a musical instrument, repairing a clock, or programming a computer.

Joseph Conrad was so preoccupied with his work while writing *Lord Jim* that one day he stood for some time in front of an open fire in his cold room, his beard on his chest and his mind in the South Seas. When he later reached a stopping point in his thoughts, he strode to his writing desk and only then discovered that the back of his dressing gown had been entirely scorched away.

Often, as in the case of Conrad that day, total absorption in a thought or activity can transcend mood and environment. Lord Macaulay, the English historian, used to walk rapidly through crowded London streets reading a book. After perusing a page, he could repeat it from memory.

Seneca, the Roman philosopher, could listen with rapt attention to a list of 2,000 disconnected words and then repeat the entire list without an error.

Blaise Pascal, John Wesley, and Robert Hall each had the ability to concentrate with such complete absorption that even the severest pain failed to disturb them or hamper their work.

Archimedes, the Greek mathematician, was so absorbed in his intricate calculations at ancient Syracuse that he first became aware of the siege of the city when he received his death wound.

In closing this section on mood and environment as aids to or detractors from concentration, let us hear from a mere mortal who also was a genius, Wolfgang Amadeus Mozart. He once wrote in a letter:

"When I am, as it were, completely myself, entirely alone, and of good cheer—say, travelling in a carriage, or walking after a good meal, or during the night when I cannot sleep; it is on such occasions that my ideas flow best and most abundantly.

"*Whence* and *how* they come, I know not; nor can I force them. Those ideas that please me I retain in memory, and am accustomed, as I have been told, to hum them to myself. If I continue in this way, it soon occurs to me how I may turn this or that morsel to account, so as to make a good dish of it, that is to say, agreeably to the rules of counterpoint, to the peculiarities of the various instruments, etc.

"All this fires my soul, and, provided I am not disturbed, my subject enlarges itself, becomes methodised and defined, and the whole, though it be long, stands almost complete and finished in my mind, so that I can survey it, like a fine picture or a beautiful statue, at a glance.

"Nor do I hear in my imagination the parts successively, but I hear them, as it were, all at once. What a delight this is I cannot tell! All this inventing, this producing, takes place in a pleasing lively dream. Still the actual hearing of the *tout ensemble* is after all the best. What has been thus produced I do not easily forget, and this is perhaps the best gift I have my Divine Maker to thank for.

"When I proceed to write down my ideas, I take out of the bag of my memory, if I may use that phrase, what has been previously collected into it in the way I have mentioned. For this reason the committing to paper is done quickly enough, for everything is, as I

131

said before, already finished; and it rarely differs on paper from what it was in my imagination.

"At this occupation I can therefore suffer myself to be disturbed; for whatever may be going on around me, I write, and even talk, but only of fowls and geese, or of Gretel or Barbel, or some such matters. But why my productions take from my hand that particular form and style that makes them Mozartish, and different from the works of other composers, is probably owing to the same cause which renders my nose so large or so aquiline, or, in short, makes it Mozart's, and different from those of other people. For I really do not study or aim at any originality."

8

Organizing Time, Work, and Thought

Whatever the task we have to perform, we can concentrate better on it if we develop good skills of organization. This often means arranging our time, work materials, and thoughts in ways that bring some logic and focus to the job we want to do.

Few people are as busy as Julia Child, "The French Chef" of television, who tells us her thoughts on concentration and organizing her work:

"There are so many different kinds of concentration and different fields in which it must be done. I think of the golf pro who must concentrate on his final putt when there are thousands of people watching and whispering around him.

"In my experience, it is very important to get peripheral and continuing things down into a habit pattern. Such as on my television programs, getting into the habit of showing things to the close-up camera, and getting into the habit of looking at the overall camera you are supposed to speak at. Although I've been at it for over fifteen years, I can still mess up on that.

"Another thing which I am not very good at but should be better at is to keep my work area in a confined square, so that I am not going out of frame, as they say. If these technical matters are mastered and become automatic, then one has time to concentrate on words and techniques.

"I never have trouble concentrating, because there is so much going on that I *have* to concentrate; it is really a question of *where* to concentrate.

"I'm sure also that it is very important, if one is to concentrate, to have a tremendous interest in what one is doing so that there is no question of having one's whole mind and soul on what one is doing."

Julia Child's problem of staying within a designated square so that she does not move out of frame on the television monitor brings up a point of organization that I find particularly helpful in concentrating as a writer: narrowing one's focus. When I have a task at hand, such as the writing of this book, I clear my work area of all other writing projects which could be distractions. The research books and files for my upcoming assignment, a book on undersea exploration, must be moved out of my field of vision. If they are in the file cabinet or on a bookshelf behind me or far off to one side where I can't see them, I won't think about *that* project and can keep my attention focused on the project at hand.

After I have blocked out all other distractions of either a visual or auditory nature, I get my work area in order with the materials I need for the task on which I intend to concentrate. I make sure the typewriter is working and has ribbon, and that correction materials are handy, along with a dictionary and necessary reference books.

When I have all else in order about me on the

desk—I prefer a big work area, so I placed two hollow core doors on some two-drawer file cabinets and created a large L-shaped desk on which I can spread out my work—I begin to attack the material I am going to use for my article or book. Usually I have a small mountain of newspaper clippings, notes, and other reference materials. At first, it all kind of overwhelms me. There is so much research material that I have to put it in some sort of logical order before I can deal with it.

The frustration in being overwhelmed by material begins to pass when I start to organize my article or book into logical parts. Each chapter of a book gets its own manila folder, its own title. Then I attack the mountain of reference material, page by page, until each item is filed in the proper folder. Finally the mountain of material is gone, filtered logically into appropriate chapters.

The next step is to arrange the material in each folder in some logical order, one subject on top of another. Once this is done with each folder or chapter, the entire book is in order, waiting to be written. The writing comes much more easily, because the material now is *organized*.

The same organization technique can be applied to just about any task. You can concentrate better on how to build a new birdhouse from an instruction booklet if you begin by putting everything else aside on your workbench. Clear the deck and focus on the instructions, pushing all empty flowerpots and other distractions off the workbench. A room can be painted faster and more efficiently if you move everything out of it and place masking tape around windows, light fixtures, and baseboards. With that done, you can concentrate on the job of painting.

Many people work hard at finding ways to avoid getting started on a project. They may run down to the drug store or supermarket, make phone calls, sharpen pencils until they're merely stubs, or brew one last cup of coffee before starting a task. Anything to postpone starting as long as possible. Hopefully, they rationalize, if they put off starting long enough, time will run out and a really legitimate excuse for procrastinating will have come along.

These invented delays are usually the result of indifference to a task, or to displeasure with it. If we are willing, we can find ways of developing genuine interest in jobs that may not basically appeal to us. Men who dislike selling often learn to enjoy their work by regarding it as a contest for awards, for incentives like vacations to the highest-seller. Housewives often can learn to tolerate, if not like, a task such as cooking or cleaning, because they look upon the work as an expression of love toward their husbands or children.

When asked how he got started each day at his writing, the German poet Goethe replied with great serenity, "Why, I just blow on my hands."

To develop the power of concentration, you must first of all learn to throw yourself into the task at hand. Yet, most of us welcome interruption because we don't realize that the unpleasant job ahead can actually absorb us, if we can simply bring ourselves to make the initial leap into it.

William James suggested that the important thing in getting started at any task is to *go through the motions*. Start making notes or sketches, or even talk to yourself about the project. Get your materials in front of you. Involve your whole person, including your body, in the job of focusing attention on the task. Your body's involvement may be slight or subtle—a matter of posture or muscular tension—but in the best efforts at concentration, it is there.

Even after we begin to concentrate on a task, there are difficulties that immediately throw themselves in front of us. A multiplicity of thoughts, half-thoughts, sounds, and impressions can crowd into our minds as if to sabotage even our best efforts.

But if we are determined, we can learn to select ruthlessly from among these many interests that present themselves demandingly for attention. Often it isn't enough just to exclude these extraneous impressions from our minds. We have to replace them with thoughts of the one thing that demands our attention. You can't push a thought out of your mind. You must always replace it with another.

Specialization is another word for concentration. When you see a mountain of work to be done, it can overwhelm you and sap your energy or frustrate you. But if you concentrate on just one part of that mountain and complete it to the exclusion of everything else, you will level the whole mountain in time.

As you tackle one thing, you probably will be troubled by a dozen other things you ought to be doing instead, things that can't wait. Or can they wait? Most of the time they can, and you know they can.

They've *got* to wait, until you or someone else can get to them.

Deciding on priorities is an extremely important part of organization. Don't scatter your priorities. Tell yourself what is important and what must wait until this task is done. It's amazing how easily satisfied your unconscious is if you keep faith with it and really give the second problem attention in turn.

This is the single-minded attitude, the one-thing-at-a-time that all of us must learn. Without it we get nowhere, either in work or in play.

Arnold Bennett, the English novelist and dramatist, described concentration as "the power to dictate to the brain its task and insure its obedience." This power comes with practice, and practice, proverbially, requires patience.

Most of us are guilty of wasting a great deal of time that could be better spent. Some people who ride a bus or train, a subway or elevated transportation to work every day waste that valuable travel time staring out a window or people-watching. Their time might be better spent in reading, which could relax them and help them to tune out the noise or other discomforts of going and coming on public transportation. Some commuters get themselves into a productive frame of mind for work by listening to music on battery-powered radios with earphones. *Do* use earphones, however, and don't distract others by forcing your sounds on them.

Kim Hunter, the Academy Award-winning actress, says that organizing her thoughts is very important in helping her concentrate on a new stage or film role:

"I suppose it boils down to a sort of yoga, blocking out everything that doesn't pertain to the task at hand. And keeping the pertinent elements *specific*."

For Archibald Cox, Harvard Law School professor and former Watergate special prosecutor, concentration is affected by a combination of things:

"The degree of interest and nearness of the deadline seem to determine the degree of my concentration."

David Franklin, who is developing techniques for teaching the deaf to "hear" through the skin, has reached the following conclusions:

"For me, the answer to concentration is in two parts. The first is time and space structure. That's easy. I need a place to work and reasonably well-defined time for work. I'm self-employed, so I supply myself a space dedicated to my work, and I define two or more days a week as dedicated to my creative efforts. I try to keep to this schedule. It doesn't matter in principle if time were set aside each day, instead of whole days, but for other reasons the schedule I've selected suits me.

"The rest of my answer is much more complex. By concentration, I am referring to the act of placing one's butt in an appropriate location and transplanting ideas and fantasies into artifacts suitable for communicating those ideas and fantasies and/or performing some function in the physical world.

"In this context, the breaking of concentration is something I experience for a number of reasons, all of which cause my mind to wander or my body to experience tension. The poorest solution I've found for this, and the one I was taught to use when I was

141

younger, was to 'force myself to concentrate.' I know of no purer way of defeating attention and exhausting one's self.

"I abandoned this system years ago and am concentrating far more effectively, but I'm not sure I can say in positive terms exactly what I've done to accomplish this. I can say, in part, some of the things I *don't* do.

"One, I don't compete. I can't worry about whether someone else is ahead of me or if my work is good enough to get public stroking. I do the best I can and this allows me to get involved with my subject instead of ego issues.

"Two, I don't worry excessively about end points while I'm working. I try to break a project up into short-term goals and focus on the immediate process. This helps to keep me focused. In a sense, I'm more of a craftsman while I'm working, and more creative when I'm sleeping, talking, and daydreaming.

"Three, I block out 'better ideas' while I'm working. Better ideas are insidious traps to give up in the face of difficulties and have a way of blurring long-term goals and stalling progress. I remember them, but I do them later.

"Four, I try not to talk too much about my work. Excessive talking tends to take the place of actual doing. There has to be a balance in this since stimulation and valuable criticism can come from other people. Still, I think most people either create or they talk about creating.

"I think what I want to say is that by focusing on specific difficulties I have in doing my work, and by taking steps to solve those difficulties, my concentration improves. It is a matter of finding harmony between one's life and one's work and maintaining the proper balance between relaxation and stress."

Ideal concentration, according to the British psychologist Eustace Miles, is of a particular nature:

It sets "first" things first and keeps them first; even while it attends to second and third things, it always has the "first" things in view.

In other words, beside the thing that is being done, the task in hand, concentration does not lose sight of the goal.

Neither does it lose sight of the things that are above and below, so to speak, and on either side of and beyond, the thing that is being done. While the pitcher on the mound has to concentrate on the strike-ball he wants to throw to the batter, he also must keep an eye on the man on first base who may try to steal second base, or the man on third who may try to make a run for home plate. The ideal concentrator has to keep his eye on the present task, yet bear in mind the things that are around him.

Miles goes on to note that ideal concentration is divertible at will. It is not simply the faculty of attending to one thing. It is, equally, the faculty of attending to any other thing, as the highest conscience directs.

Ideal concentration comes without physical tension. During effective concentration of the mind, the muscles must be under control for the sake of effectiveness, economy, and gracefulness.

One of the things that so impressed many people about Napoleon was the power and persistence of his attention. He could work for eighteen hours at a stretch, whether it would be on one piece of work or several in turn. His mind would never waver. He would not be distracted from one subject by another, neglecting the matter at hand for one which he would consider turning to next. No one was ever more wholly immersed in what he was doing, it is said, and no one ever made a better allocation of his time among all the things he had to do.

Napoleon wrote that he kept various ideas and affairs arranged in his head "as in a wardrobe."

"When I wish to put any matter out of my mind, I close its drawer and open the drawer belonging to another," Napoleon has said. "The contents of the drawers never get mixed, and they never worry me or weary me. Do I want to sleep? I close all the drawers, and then I am asleep."

Never was there a brain so disciplined and so adaptable, so ready at all moments for any task, so capable of sudden and complete concentration as Napoleon's, says H. A. Taine, one of his early biographers.

Most of us can improve our concentration if we follow the advice of Alan Lakein, the noted time-management consultant. Lakein keeps a "To Do" list. The first thing he believes we should do upon arriving at our place of work in the morning is to make a list of what we want to accomplish that day. Items should be arranged in order of priority. During the day we should attend to each item in turn and cross it off the list as it is completed, perhaps adding others that might occur to us during the course of the day. In the evening, we should check to see how many of the items written down still remain undone, then give ourselves a score. Our goal should be to cross off every single item in each day's "To Do" list.

Lakein maintains that in his years of research, the one difference he has found between people at the top of the success ladder and those at the bottom is that those at the top use a "To Do" list every day, organizing priorities for the best use of their time. Those at the bottom do not keep such lists.

Benjamin Franklin is famous for having followed the concept that we can best attack the whole by dealing with its parts when the whole may be too difficult a task to attempt at once. He found this method very useful when he was trying to acquire virtue. He said it was easier to acquire individual virtues (which are the parts of virtue) each in turn than to acquire virtue as a whole. He couldn't concentrate on the whole, but he could more easily concentrate on each part in turn. Franklin describes his plan in detail in his *Autobiography*.

Franklin's "To Do" list for virtue, many of whose items are good general concentration aids, is as follows:

1. Temperance—Eat not to dullness; drink not to elevation.

2. Silence—Speak not but what may benefit others or yourself; avoid trifling conversation.

3. Order—Let all your things have their places; let each part of your business have its time.

4. Resolution—Resolve to perform what you ought; perform without fail what you resolve.

5. Frugality—Make no expense but to do good to others or yourself; that is, waste nothing.

6. Industry—Lose no time; be always employed in

something useful; cut off all unnecessary actions.

7. Sincerity—Use no hurtful deceit; think innocently and justly; and, if you speak, speak accordingly.

8. Justice—Wrong none by doing injuries or omitting the benefits that are your duty.

9. Moderation—Avoid extremes; forbear resenting injuries, so much as you think they deserve.

10. Cleanliness—Tolerate no uncleanliness in body, clothes, or habitation.

11. Tranquility—Be not disturbed at trifles or at accidents common or unavoidable.

12. Chastity.

13. Humility—Imitate Jesus and Socrates.

Said Franklin by way of explaining his list:

"My intention being to acquire the habitude of all these virtues, I judged it would be well not to distract my attention by attempting the whole at once, but to fix it on *one* of them at a time; and when I should be master of that, then to proceed to another; and so on till I should have gone through the thirteen."

Fanklin determined to give a week's strict attention to each of the virtues successively, thus giving himself a deadline. Apparently, Franklin eventually was satisfied that he had scored well after many weeks had passed. But he also maintained that even in failure, there is virtue in attempting each of the thirteen virtues.

Organization was one of the secrets of Benjamin Franklin's incredible success in a wide variety of fields, from inventing to statesmanship. If we can emulate his ability to organize, we can begin to draw upon the power of concentration which helped him to achieve so much in his busy life.

9

How to Train
Your Memory

Harry Houdini, the legendary magician, had phenomenal powers of concentration, which he sharpened via memory-training exercises with his son. They would take a walk, enter a shop to look at its contents, and then play a game of trying to recall everything they had seen. When they began playing the game, they could recall only a few things from the store. But soon they were able to recall everything.

The next time you enter an appliance store, look around at what is there. Then close your eyes and see how much you can remember. Or, while you are waiting for a light to change at an intersection, look around you and then close your eyes. Try to remember what your eyes and mind have taken in.

Robert L. Montgomery of St. Paul, Minnesota, a leading researcher into memory training, says that 85 percent of everything we comprehend and remember is learned through the eyes. Only 11 percent is obtained through the ears, and just 3 or 4 percent of what we remember comes from taste, touch, or smell.

Why is it that most people can remember all the words to a popular song they knew while in high school, but then in college have trouble remembering the chemistry lecture they heard only the day before?

Montgomery says it is because our visual capacity—the ability to retain pictures and patterns, including musical and rhyming patterns, is far more efficient than our verbal memory capacity, the ability to recall words.

"Desire is a prerequisite to memory," says Montgomery, "and a prerequisite to memory is concentration. Retention is dependent upon attention.

"Most of us just have to force ourselves to concentrate. There's really no other way to do it.

"Einstein admitted that thinking is the hardest thing we can do. You have to *prepare* for concentration, for listening, for thinking, by removing all distractions. Forget bill-paying, stress, noise from airplanes, when you have to draw upon your memory.

"Take notes. You can help remember more if you put down an agenda for the day or for a meeting you are holding or attending, highlighting key and essential points to remember.

"The Orientals say a picture is worth a thousand words, and I agree. One time *seeing* is worth a thousand times *hearing*. We achieve 71 percent greater retention through *seeing* than we do when writing things down. This is one reason why audio-visual learning methods have become so popular and proven to be such effective training tools in schools and business.

"If you prepare properly for concentration and memory and listening and reading by blocking out as many internal and external distractions as possible, your powers in achieving mastery of over those skills will increase dramatically. But most of us will do just about anything to avoid thinking or concentrating.

We will take advantage of or invent any excuse we can, to keep us away from concentrating on a difficult or perhaps unpleasant task as long as we can, hoping it might go away and we won't have to attend to it at all."

Do you have trouble remembering names of people when you meet them socially, at school, or at work? Try this technique for name-recalling used by Harry Lorayne, memory expert and co-author of *The Memory Book* (with Jerry Lucas).

Forgetting names, says Lorayne, is simply a matter of not getting them, not hearing them, in the first place. His system for remembering people involves three steps. Catch the name, study the person's face, and then combine the two into such a ridiculous fashion that you'll never forget them.

For example, at a party, you are introduced to a young woman named Doxsee. Let her name register in your mind for a moment by visualizing it. Her name could remind you of a dock and the sea, so in your mind you could identify her as "Miss Dock-Sea."

Next, take this name substitute you have created in your mind and concentrate on Miss Doxsee's face. Decide which of her facial features is the most interesting or outstanding, whether it is her pug nose, narrow forehead, dimples, buck teeth, or anything that will remind you of her. The combination of making a visual word image from the name and looking for an identifiable facial characteristic ought to greatly help you remember the name.

Jogging may help us develop greater powers of memory, according to Dr. John Cacioppe of Notre Dame

College in Ohio. He says his tests have shown that joggers think more efficiently after their heart rates have been accelerated through exercise. This could mean that jogging or participating in other vigorous sports can heighten our mental output.

Cacioppe's research indicates that a slight increase in the heart rate corresponds with improved performance on multiple-choice tests. It also seems to enhance the ability to organize thoughts and arrange evidence in oral arguments.

In his study called *Stop Forgetting*, Dr. Bruno Furst, another authority on memory-enhancing, says that memory exercises cannot be separated from exercises in observation, concentration, and imagination. He suggests that whenever we try to remember something new by connecting it with something we already know (as in the "Dock-Sea" method), we must use our imagination to form an association. We must concentrate on both items in order to impress them upon our mind.

Most people's powers of observation are poorly developed, says Dr. Furst. We don't really observe what we see or hear. We can improve our ability in this area if we train our five senses to the task. Since taste and smell play less important roles in observation for most of us, the other three senses are the ones to focus on—sight, hearing, and touch.

Dr. Furst suggests that to train the eyes to observe better we should put into play a little artwork. Look at an object, such as a telephone or an automobile. Study it closely for a few minutes. Then wait about an hour and try to make a drawing of the object on paper, without taking a new look at it. Compare the drawing with the original, notice any mistakes, and then make a new sketch of the object without taking a new look at it.

Similarly, look at a picture in a book or magazine and observe as many details as possible. Then redraw the picture from memory. If you can't draw well, do the exercise with a friend and ask him to put questions to you regarding details of the picture.

Look about the room you are in while you are reading this. Notice what is in the room and where it is located. Then write down what you remember from what you have seen. But challenge yourself a little. Don't settle for recording that there is a bookcase in the room. Try to recall how many shelves are in the bookcase, how many books are on each shelf, what some of the titles are, and so on.

Train yourself to estimate distances and quantities. While taking a walk, estimate the number of feet it may take to get from your front door to your car, or to a tree in the distance. Count your steps and check your judgment. When passing a store window, estimate the number of items on display. Then count and check on your estimate.

In training the ear to observe and to remember better what you hear, Dr. Furst suggests that you begin by identifying noises around you at home or work. Some of the noises may come from within the house or workplace while others may come from outside. Listen to the sounds and attempt to identify them. This can help train your ears to hear better when you listen to a speaker.

As for training observation in touch, close your eyes and touch various objects with your fingers. Decide what kind of material they are made of. Estimate their weight or determine their shape.

It also is helpful to develop our skills in classifying things, using our memory as a filing system. Write down a list of twenty words, such as *book, milk, dog, rose,* etc. Number them from one to twenty. Look at the list for no more than twenty seconds, then put it aside and try to see how many of them you can remember.

Next, look at the words again, this time noticing that they can be grouped into various classes. The sample words above might be divided into four categories: reading materials, foods, pets, and flowers.

Learning to identify and classify sharpens our powers of observation and increases our ability to remember.

Repetition is another useful tool for improving memory. Repetition can be likened to a path in the mind, connecting the ideas and binding them together, so the flow of thought travels easily along the beaten track. Repetition and practice make muscular movements easier and more economical. The same is true with the mind. Every part of the body does a thing more easily when the task becomes habitual.

Some lucky people have what is called a photographic memory. They are able to recall information instantly and almost totally after absorbing it only briefly. Unfortunately, most of us do not possess that ability.

Researchers surmise that we probably had photographic memories when we were children, but eventually grew out of them. Nearly one-fourth of all children under the age of ten possesses this ability to look at something—such as a printed page—and then read it back as if looking at a photo of it.

But photographic recall tends to fade, for some reason, by the end of adolescence. It is believed that we lose this ability because when we were children, it didn't perform any particular function for us. Like an unused muscle, whatever caused us to have photographic memories fell into disuse and we lost it.

Other researchers are looking into the possibility that gender plays an important part in what we remember. A recent test at the University of Washington revealed that among subjects participating as witnesses to crimes, male witnesses are more likely than female witnesses to remember any men involved in the crime. Furthermore, female witnesses are likely to recall participants in crimes who are women.

Elizabeth F. Loftus, a University of Washington psychologist who conducted the study, reports that leading questions can influence the memory of male and female witnesses. Women clearly remember more "female" items such as the actions and descriptions of the main female characters in the crime. The details men remembered more clearly involved the "male" items such as the main male character or an automobile used in the crime.

Further research in this memory study might aid judges and juries in becoming better able to interpret conflicting testimony.

One of the best and longest-used techniques for

remembering better is the art of mnemonics. It all began centuries ago in Greece when the poet Simonides attended a banquet one afternoon with a large number of guests. While he was temporarily called away, an earthquake shook the area and all the celebrants at the banquet were crushed beneath rock and rubble.

Relatives of the victims were sorely grieved since, after the wreckage was removed, it was impossible to tell who was who. Simonides solved the identity crisis by simply remembering where each guest had sat around the banquet table. He was so impressed with his own memory that he founded the art of mnemonic techniques. His specific technique is known as the method of loci, association of places.

Simonides' technique works like this . . . If you have a speech to make, say on modern communication, draw word-picture associations from things you see as you walk to school or work. As you pass a telephone booth, associate it with the first point you intend to make in your speech, about high telephone rates. Next, as you pass a park, you may see a newspaper being blown against a tree, which can remind you to talk next about newspapers and their competition with television for a share of the news market. Finally, you may see or imagine a bee buzzing about some flowers at the base of a tree by some fallen leaves. This situation can help you to remember your conclusion (bee-leaf = belief; puns often are used in mnemonics). Using this technique of object and place association can reportedly help you remember as many as sixty to seventy separate ideas.

Another area of research in memory involves the distinction between short-term memory and long-term memory.

Short-term memory refers to the means by which information is retained in the mind for immediate use, such as telephone numbers we may have to remember only until we dial them. Afterward we can forget such items because we may never use them again. The information we retain in short-term memory is not a complete image of the events that have taken place at the sensory level. Short-term memory seems to retain the immediate *interpretation* of those events. By constantly repeating short-term information, we can maintain the information for an indefinite length of time. This ability to keep things active in short-term memory by rehearsal of the information is considered one of the most important characteristics of the memory system.

Long-term memory is regarded as the most important of the memory systems. It involves your need to remember things like your Social Security number without hesitation. Everything that must be retained in the mind for more than just a few minutes at a time is stored in our long-term memory. Problems in long-term memory come mainly from retrieval difficulties.

Dr. Robert Bostrom and his colleagues at the Department of Communication of the University of Kentucky in Lexington are studying short-term and long-term implications in speech.

"We have discovered that people are different in their short-term vs. long-term ability to take information in from running speech," says Dr. Bostrom. "One study shows that the way these things behave is quite

157

different from the kind of research people do of short-term and long-term memory.

"In other words, short-and-long-term *listening* seems to behave quite differently. Redundant material doesn't make a difference, for one thing. Repetitions make a difference with memory, but not in listening.

"When we categorized our students into good conversationalists and good speakers, as opposed to bad conversationalists and bad speakers, we found that they were about the same in long-term listening, such as listening to lectures. But they were really different in short-term listening. Our good subjects are short-term listeners and conversationalists.

"We don't know what causes this—why a good short-term listener may be a good conversationalist. Maybe it's simply because they can take it in and assimilate the things they hear and then drop them— forget them—as the conversation goes on.

"We even tried to break their concentration by distracting them on purpose, to see if they could achieve these results even under distractions. But it didn't seem to interfere significantly.

"We did do one study which seemed to prove that their concentration improved if they were fearful of getting a bad grade in the course because of a bad grade on the testing project. Fear of failure seemed to make them try harder to avoid something bad.

"But I don't think that in our day-to-day conversations most of us have this fear, although there are some people who are really shy and fear failure in speaking situations."

Meanwhile, scientists who are always looking for

ways of putting things in pill form, so we can become instantly slimmer or healthier, now are working on producing a "memory pill."

Preliminary findings suggest that such a pill could enable us to remember more so we would become smarter. It also could help us recall things we may have repressed psychologically, which could aid us in dealing better with our mental hang-ups. The memory pill also could retrieve information which in older people may have been pushed into oblivion by senility.

Psychiatric researchers at the National Institute of Mental Health (NIMH) say such a pill could be taken to help us do well on examinations, recall names and dates and telephone numbers, or to perform tasks requiring a great deal of memorization.

It has been discovered that a drug similar to a naturally-occurring brain chemical greatly increases learning and memory in both normal people and in those suffering from such mental disorders as depression.

Progress in laboratory tests has been so successful that according to Dr. Herbert Weingartner of NIMH's Laboratory of Psychology and Psychopathology, chemicals may be produced in the next five to ten years that could improve learning and memory.

A second type of memory pill involves lecithin, a substance found in many foods, which shows evidence of helping revive memory in senile patients.

Over the last few years, the discovery of dozens of brain chemicals called neurotransmitters has given scientists new insight into the complex and mysterious workings of brain cells as well as providing clues about how researchers can manipulate the brain. Among other things, drugs are being tested that could help the brain cells function for longer periods of time.

But like all wonder drugs which may be "just around the corner" of discovery and general use, a memory pill is still really only a dream waiting to come true. In the meantime, if we hope to improve our memory we will have to work a little harder at the task.

The techniques in this chapter and elsewhere throughout the book can help us train ourselves to remember more and better.

10

Learning from Eastern Disciplines of Meditation

Highly-increased technology of the past century which was supposed to simplify life and make it more manageable for us has actually intensified the stress we must cope with in our daily lives. Stress results in loss of concentration, decreased productivity, and numerous physical and emotional impairments. We become easily frustrated and find that even small tasks are difficult to think out, to reckon with.

The very fact that many of us get frustrated because we are unable to find the time or techniques which would allow us to mentally relax and concentrate—to reach some level of satisfying equilibrium in our daily lives—adds more stress and compounds the problem. As many of us rely on electronic equipment to do our work, solve our problems, and provide our relaxation, we tend to get farther away from an ability to draw upon our own inner resources to find tranquility and contentment.

But the more we avoid looking inward for both the strength and calm we need in order to cope, the less practice we have in finding the calm within us.

Techniques used to achieve a form of mental relaxation have traditionally been associated with religious teachings of the East, where for centuries they have

been an essential part of everyday living. However, in the past two or three decades there has been a dramatic increase in the use of meditative techniques among peoples in the Western world, both for relaxation and to increase concentration and awareness.

The word *meditation* is often difficult or uncomfortable for many of us to consider objectively, because it tends to connote exotic Eastern cults or the practices of some Christian monks who devote a large part of their lives to contemplation of some Supreme Being. How often have you heard someone complain that a yogi or a monk is "merely contemplating his navel."

As Dr. Robert E. Ornstein notes in his book *The Psychology of Consciousness,* Western culture with its impersonal, objective scientific approach and its strong emphasis on logic and analysis, often makes it difficult for many people to conceive of a psychological method based on the existence of another, intuitive mode of thought.

As far as "contemplating one's navel," many of the Eastern religions and martial arts recommend concentrating on a key point in the body, usually around the navel, from which both psychological and physical power reportedly come. The aikido expert can accomplish great feats of strength by focusing the flow of *ki* to parts of his body. Energy is directed through any part of the body on which he focuses his attention and concentration. When the aikido expert lets his mind rest at "the one point," a spot about two inches behind the navel, he can be simultaneously calm and almost immovable.

In a sense, meditation begins where concentration

ends. The express purpose of concentration is to focus all of one's attention upon a small field of mental vision. In this type of mental focusing, our general and active awareness is at its highest level.

Such a level of concentration involves narrowing the field of mental vision, while in meditation an overall expansion of the mental field is involved. As Earnest Wood pointed out in his book, *Mind and Memory Training*, "In concentration you gain clear vision; in meditation you try to keep that clear vision, but extend it over a larger field and into depths and heights of thought which you have not been able to reach clearly before."

What we attempt to develop in meditation is an expanded mind which can grasp a great deal of information and knowledge at once while remaining capable of effectively integrating the material and dealing decisively with the whole.

Man is particularly well-suited for this task, mainly because of his unique attributes of *memory*, which allow him to continually store new information and new images, and *reflection*, by which he can consider this newly-acquired material in order to determine just how it relates to any previous knowledge.

As a result, clear impressions observed by the concentrating mind can immediately become the material for that mind to work upon through meditation. Success in meditation therefore implies success in concentration, and the factors which are conducive to this— relaxation of the body, a quiet environment, and emotional calm—are also conducive to effective and satisfying meditation.

165

Just as concentration leads on to meditation, so does meditation lead on to *contemplation*, which can be defined as concentration at the extreme end of one's line of thought.

After a great amount of concentration and meditation has been successfully applied to a task or concept, there is a point at which you can benefit from stopping the regular flow of thought to dwell for a short time—in a calm and somewhat detached frame of mind—upon the achievements and ideas that you have come upon. You may have reached a level or depth of thought beyond which you cannot go on to gain additional insight. At this point you can stop thinking actively and reflect contentedly on the most important facts, and at the highest levels, that you have attained. This aspect of contemplation can follow the processes of intense concentration and relaxed meditation.

Such contemplation can create new and higher levels on which consciousness and mental awareness can stand. As a result, when you come around again to deal with deep concentration and the thoughts that evolve from it, you will find that it is easier to grasp these thoughts. Then the meditative process can be carried still further.

In order to attain a systematic approach to contemplation, a two-step process should be followed—

1) The *attention* must be directly centered on the object/concept; and, 2) The mind must remain actively centered on the object/concept while its ordinary activities cease.

In this final stage of contemplation, one can stop all

comparing and reasoning, keeping the attention fixed actively upon the object/concept while making a concerted effort to see in the vagueness and uncertainty something more definite and tangible. For the time being, you refuse to drop to the ordinary regions of conscious activity in which your sight is clear and concise. It is at this level that you regain your concentration, but this time you regain it at the highest plane of your line of thought.

All of the meditation practices, including yoga, Zen meditation, and Transcendental Meditation—and all the martial arts such as karate, judo, aikido, jiu-jitsu, kung fu, tae-kwan do, etc.—attempt to aid the individual in: 1) Reaching a more relaxed state, 2) Increasing the ability to concentrate, 3) Raising mental and physical awareness, and 4) Attaining a higher level of thinking activity and/or consciousness.

It is generally agreed that there are three major types of meditation practices. These can be distinguished by their different methods of mental focus. There are those meditations with an external object of focus (a lighted candle or natural object); meditations with an internal focus (a mental image or thought); and meditations that have no fixed focus.

Similarly, these meditations can be further classified as *concentration* practices and *mindfulness* practices. The concentration practice in which we are most interested involves techniques for focusing attention on a particular target. Such techniques are included in the first two categories, involving either an external or internal focus. In contrast, the mindfulness practice simply involves observation and recognition of whatever comes into one's mental awareness.

Common to all of these meditative practices, and embracing the variety of experiences that occur during meditation, is the notion of *passive awareness*. This is a state in which the mind becomes still and consciousness actually transcends the thought process. *Awareness* describes the focus of one's attention on the present moment and the mental experiences that are occurring, while the word *passive* emphasizes that no specific action must be taken in order to experience in this way. One must merely be open and allow the experience to occur.

A basic principle of any form of meditation is the notion that passive awareness is a natural, primary, and direct form of experience that is ordinarily overshadowed and obscured by the constant activity of the mind. The purpose of this type of concentrative meditation, therefore, is to allow the mind to become relaxed and quiet, and hence to discover its capacity for this further development and mental experience.

The meditative procedures used to achieve this state of passive awareness can be practiced with relative simplicity and do not involve a long training period. They merely require a small degree of self-discipline and the desire to be alone, to relax your mind from its constant and sometimes hectic activity, and to experience the attitude of passive awareness.

Meditation first requires that you find a quiet environment and a comfortable sitting position. A nice outdoor setting such as a wooded area is ideal, but even a quiet backyard or porch will do. The point is to find a location or room where you can remove yourself from possible distractions and therefore help your concentration on the meditative action.

To rid the mind of its own activity and internal chatter it helps to initiate a series of deep breaths through the nostrils while simultaneously removing the tongue from the roof of the mouth. As you perform this rhythm of inhaling and exhaling deeply, try to focus your attention at the tip of the nostrils and to quietly "see" the air flowing in and out past the tip of each nostril.

You may want to count your long, deep breaths (on the exhale), in order to aid your concentration. Try particularly hard on the exhale to relax every part of the body in which you feel any type of nervous tension. It is sometimes helpful, when beginning, to purposefully tense the muscles of the arms and legs while inhaling on your first few breaths. Then let the tension totally flow from every part of your body, including your mind, while you exhale as fully as possible.

The repetition of a particular sound or word, known by Hindus as the *mantra*, also can be useful in helping the mind to relax and concentrate on the internal object or thought of focus. The mind slowly follows the lulling sensation of the mantra or silent counting of the breaths to gradually quieter levels of mental activity.

There is an increased satisfaction associated with this quiet, calming mental activity. The process can be thought of as taking place in three stages: First, the mind is focused and begins experiencing an object or thought. Second, this thought begins to fade, as the mind passes through various levels of feeling and thinking. (It is at this stage that all distracting thoughts must be eliminated.) Third, all thoughts fade, which leaves the mind alone with itself in the state of passive awareness, or oneness. The mind remains undisturbed, aware in itself, for as long as we can hold the experience.

The feeling can be associated with that of having the tension and cluttered mental activity massaged away from the crevices of the mind—a form of mind-clearing. There is a renewed sense of inner serenity and blissful consciousness. Further observation of the meditative process reveals that energy and concentration increase as we experience these quieter levels of the thinking process.

Our most useful and creative ideas arise when our mind is quiet. We often struggle with a problem or task for days, until finally we sit down and relax or take our mind off of it. Then we invariably note a powerful solution surfacing as a thought. It seems then that the closer we come to practicing and experiencing the most quiet aspect of the meditative process, the more energy, concentration, and intelligence we find in our everyday thinking.

The essence of meditation is an initial concentration on a pattern in the mind or a pleasant thought. Try pretending you are sitting on a mountaintop or near the oceanside. Imagine a sense of calmness and tranquility. It is best to begin the practice of meditation with the eyes closed, while focusing your attention on these internal thoughts.

You should attempt to practice this method once a day for at least a week, until you begin to feel a type of self-induced emotional calmness. Once you begin to truly experience this "joyful stillness of the mind," you will notice the inner calm that results.

It may take up to eight or ten attempts at the meditation method to achieve this, depending on your state of mind, your mood and the environment around you, and your own ability to prevent distracting thoughts from interfering with this practice. Realizing meditation's positive effects in aiding your overall concentration, you will want to practice regularly and experience this somewhat different mode of thinking.

Since our usual thinking process is mostly concerned with events happening outside of ourselves—including our emotional attachments, social interactions, and our feelings and sensory contacts—we are constantly diverting our thinking and general concentration toward these external factors. Meditation can be looked upon as an attempt by each individual to refocus his or her outwardly-directed consciousness inward, where it can aid effective concentration.

As you learn to concentrate more easily and productively with the aid of meditation, the rate at which you expend your body's energy resources will be noticeably lowered. You should begin to feel much more mentally active and less physically exhausted at the end of the day. If you practice twice a day for fifteen to twenty minutes, usually before eating any breakfast and then once again before dinner, you will experience the best results.

After the mental sensation of meditation has been achieved successfully on a regular basis, and the subsequent general awareness and increased ability to concentrate becomes more evident to you, you can practice whenever you feel the need to mentally relax and experience passive awareness.

Along with the increased awareness and perception that a systematic program of concentration and meditation can bring about comes the accompanying ability to think more creatively. Numerous artists, writers, and poets have described their own enhanced creative powers after having achieved a meditative-type experience.

The major physiological change we experience from meditation is a decrease in the rate of metabolism. This is called hypometabolism and results in a restful state which taxes bodily energy resources less than usual. Also during meditation, the brain's alpha waves (slow brain waves) increase in intensity and frequency, and so far we know that alpha waves are present when people feel relaxed. Meditation also relaxes us so we consume less oxygen, which can reduce work of the heart. And meditation increases the Galvanic Skin Response (GSR) during relaxation, while GSR decreases with anxiety or stress.

William Wordsworth, the English poet laureate, believed that every man could attain the vision of joy and harmony of life in nature, which for him transformed the meaning of his entire existence. His poems often are described as a series of private investigations devoted to the detailed explanation of how this vision might be achieved.

Wordsworth's described method of attaining this meditative condition emphasizes the regular practice of a passive attitude. If man can divorce himself from all the distracting objects, petty cares and desires, and distressing situations which often surround him, he can more easily reach an equilibrium of "wise passiveness." A deliberate cessation of the mind's intellectual activities and basic desires could be effectively used to reach this condition.

Wordsworth felt that with habitual training, one could experience the "central peace subsisting forever at the heart of endless agitation." His description of this experience can be found in these lines from *Tintern Abbey*:

> . . . that serene and blessed mood,
> In which . . . the breath of this corporeal frame,
> And even the motion of our human blood
> Almost suspended, we are laid asleep
> In body, and become a living soul:
> While with an eye made quiet by the power
> Of harmony, and the deep power of joy,
> We see into the life of things.

11

Exercises to Help You Concentrate

A five-year-old boy in a small Michigan town stopped on his way to kindergarten one morning recently to play on a pile of eighteen-foot lengths of cast-iron pipes stacked near the schoolyard. While he was standing on the pipes, one of them began to roll down and the boy fell under it.

A motorist passing by stopped his car when he heard the screams of some teenage girls who saw the boy get trapped beneath the heavy pipe. Arnold Lemerand, the motorist, had been warned by his doctor not to exert himself by lifting heavy objects after suffering a heart attack a few years before. But when Lemerand heard the screams and saw the situation, he instantly ran over to help.

"I just walked over, picked the pipe up, and the girls dragged the boy out of there," says Lemerand. "When I picked the pipe off of him, I thought it must weigh 300 or 400 pounds."

When Lemerand went back later, he couldn't budge the pipe and neither could his grown sons, for in fact the pipe he had lifted off the boy weighed 1,800 pounds.

"God just had to have given him a surge of strength," says Patricia Toth, the mother of the boy, Philip.

175

"That's why my son is alive today."

Weightlifters often concentrate intently before attempting to lift heavy weights. Arnold Lemerand says all his attention at the moment he went to lift the pipe off Philip Toth was focused on one thing—saving the boy's life by taking the pipe off him—without regard for how much the pipe might weigh.

Whether it was a miracle, an act of God giving Lemerand the strength he needed at that moment, or just Lemerand's ability to concentrate on lifting the pipe, we'll never know. The incident in either case goes down as another incredible example of how we can meet a test if we put our minds to it—if we concentrate on the task before us and block out all other thoughts including ifs, ands, and maybes.

To every one of life's goals, the shortcut is concentration. No matter what the goal ahead of us may be, the first step is to find and follow the path of concentration.

"Out of the blind thicket of human destiny that surrounds, tangles and impedes the great majority of us," Edward Earle Purinton, a pioneer in efficiency studies, has said, "the one clear, open, swift way to freedom is the path of concentration."

What do you need most? *Health—money—power—leisure—friends—counselors—advantages—opportunities?* Learn to concentrate, and whatever you need most will come to you. The law never fails.

Purinton defined concentration as "the science of knowing what we want most to do, have and be; the art of achieving it; and the habit of forgetting it."

The prime essential is a fixed goal. Purinton used

the example of the racing crew of a big Eastern university. Every member of the crew knows just where he must end the race and land the boat. He has learned to time his stroke to the fraction of a second. He has stripped away every ounce of superfluous clothing. He has for weeks lived with the thought of racing and winning as his primary reasons for being. He has fully mastered the principles and methods of teamwork.

Such concentration and dedication can be applied to any goal we have in life, says Purinton, who suggests we ask ourselves—

"Just where am I going to be at the end of the race of life, or five, or ten, or twenty years from now? Have I a definite picture of the goal in my mind? Have I chosen, and proved, the shortest, easiest, and best way to that goal?

"Am I working every day, every hour, with this goal in view? Are all the useless things left behind? Is every act in my working hours properly, regularly timed, so that my daily output is sure to equal my maximum?

"Do all my habits of life speed me on to my goal—or do some of them handicap and distract me? Is every one of my working associates eager to help me win? If not, why not—and where am I now? Have I advanced all that was possible? Do I know the causes of my slowness in progressing? How shall I remove the obstacles, in my surroundings and myself?

"These are a few of the questions for every alert man or woman to face bravely and settle fairly, as initial steps on the road of concentration."

Before attempting to concentrate, you should have your greatest, finest, strongest desire in mind and designate the exact goal you want to reach through concentration. Then line up your present system of work, thought, and private life with your ultimate goal to such an extent that you can see how every move you take moves you forward.

Next, make your will a power so firm, prompt, and irresistible, that you do precisely and fully whatever you set out to do. Now you are prepared to learn to concentrate.

A secretary, Purinton suggests, can make her first concentration exercise the desire to make every letter, manuscript, and memorandum *perfect*, so as not to waste a moment of her boss's time in the location and correction of her mistakes. After making every piece of work faultless during a whole day, she can try it for two days, three days, a week. After attaining a perfect record for a week, she can then focus speed. Without losing in accuracy, it should be possible to gain perhaps 30 percent in rapidity, merely by ceaseless practice in mental and manual concentration.

After achieving success in speed and accuracy, the next objective is to find an easier way of doing the work you have made better and faster. Modifications of scientific management and new equipment can quite possibly save you needless motions and aid in concentration and productivity. Promotion, says Purinton, follows concentration.

"All great people are masters of concentration," Purinton maintains. "And any man or woman will be successful when they have learned to be masters of concentration. The texture of the brain counts for little; the size of the brain counts for less. The *use* of the brain is the measure of human power.

"Concentration is merely intensive farming of the mind; and what the scientific farmer can do for and with his crops, the scientific thinker can do for and with his *thoughts*. We have today the new agriculture, we shall have tomorrow the new menticulture. The barren mind, as the barren field, is merely one that has not been cultivated. And the output of any mind, as of any field, can be doubled by the right methods of cultivation."

Here are ten guides which can aid us on our path toward greater concentration and higher achievement in our work:

1. *Focus of taste and talent.* Always concentrate on what you want to achieve and may reasonably hope to do well in a determined length of time. The first move in concentration is to find out what you are meant to be, then the prime focus of your will should be to achieve that goal.

2. *A clear, firm, and useful ambition, both immediate and ultimate.* The world's most powerful camera is the human mind; a picture of our desired achievement— mental photography—can focus our minds on our goal.

3. *A surplus of energy, and control of the sources of vitality.* The mind that creates must be a self-renewing dynamo of impelling, animating, electrifying thought. Physical health is the basis. Whether you put your whole self into your brain and evolve a masterpiece of music or invention, or whether you put your whole self into your fingers and weave a rare fabric or weld the steel frame of a fifty-story building, your power of

179

concentration depends on how healthy you are. Eat, exercise, and sleep with vitality in mind.

4. *A regular concentration habit, both manual and mental.* If you are ill and confined to bed for days or weeks, after you are well and up and around again, you may feel you can hardly walk. To walk right, you must walk every day. So it is that to think right, you must think every day, and toward a given point or goal. Learn to spend at least a half-hour each day fostering and strengthening your life purpose by a period of intense, original, constructive thought on the best and quickest ways of reaching your goal. And form the habit of doing *everything* promptly, thoroughly, and scientifically.

5. *A proper observance of time and place.* For concentration of mind, the best time seems to be the early morning, when the brain is clearest, the body strongest. The best place is wherever you can find silence and solitude.

6. *Pay strict attention to the physiology of thought.* A ready supply of rich, pure blood to the brain is an essential to powerful thought. Don't try to concentrate when physically tired, or less than two hours after a full meal. Give brain and nerve foods a large place in your diet. Don't wear constricting clothes that can congest the blood and retard its passage to the brain.

7. *A systematic study of practical psychology.* A thinker must know the mind as an electrical engineer knows the dynamo, not for the sake of theoretical knowledge, but so as to get the greatest service out of the mechanism.

8. *A balanced life.* The strain of holding the mind in

tension must be offset by frequent periods of absolute relaxation, whether through sport, a long walk, gardening, listening to music or practicing a musical instrument, etc.

9. *A dauntless perseverance.* No matter how long your goal may take to achieve, holding to your purpose makes you strong. Ten thousand obstacles may stand in your way, but you are stronger than any of these blocks. You can learn to survive success if you learn how to survive failure.

10. *A never-failing fund of optimism.* The road of concentration is not necessarily a superhighway of roses. Concentration is the science of removing the word *can't* from the mind. When this has been performed—this necessary operation on the intellect— such a new array of opportunities will manifest itself that no pessimist can live in its presence.

"Become an optimist now," says Purinton, "that you may feel at home with the successful workers when they gather at the goal of their ambitions. Only the optimist *sees* opportunities. And the road of concentration is the world's highway of opportunities."

Like Benjamin Franklin's list of thirteen steps to achieve virtue, mentioned earlier in this essay, Purinton's ten steps to greater concentration cannot be achieved overnight. We may progress in mastering some of the steps to various degrees at various times and our ability to concentrate and learn may improve. At other times it will seem to depart us.

Steady effort to improve our skills in thinking, listening, and reading, will result in steady mastery of the power to concentrate better. Improvement we realize in concentration will be fed back into our subconscious, creating a chain reaction. Our self-image and self-confidence will increase to help us overcome new obstacles to concentration.

Some researchers in concentration suggest that a good exercise is to see things as if you were deaf and dumb, and had no power of taste or smell. Or concentrate on sounds, or try to "see things as if you were blind." Blind people are said to "see" with their ears. They identify people with their ears just as surely as we identify them with our eyes.

When you listen to music, pick out one of the parts, such as the bass; or while listening to an orchestra, pick out an instrument, such as the violin. Shut your ears to all other instruments; concentrate on that one instrument alone. That is an advanced exercise in aural concentration.

Most of us can invent our own exercises to help us concentrate better with our eyes, our ears, our senses of touch and taste, if we use our imaginations. In order to have vivid imagination, it is said that one needs a mind stocked with real sense-impressions. The first step toward training the imagination is to observe the realities of life, to recall them immediately and then at intervals afterward, and to establish them in the memory.

Out of these impressions of reality we can make up our own imagination, altering the realities or the memories of them to form new pictures. But in order to observe and realize, we must train all of our senses.

To stimulate our imaginations and improve our powers of concentration, the following exercises are suggested by Ernest E. Wood, authority on mind and memory training:

1. Look about the room you are in right now, observing all the little things it contains. Close your eyes and visualize all the objects you have seen as they now pass before your mind in imagination, until the last of them has passed.

2. Imagine yourself taking a walk, noticing all the details along a familiar road or street as you pass by. Then visually return the same way, remembering what you passed from last to first.

3. Pass in imagination through some previous experience you've had, to recall as much of it as you can. Or at the end of the day, think back on everything you did that day in reverse order from going to bed to getting up that morning.

4. Concentrate on a sight or sound about you, such as the ticking of a clock. Ask yourself the cause of that sound, tracing back the causes as far as possible, until you have thought upon all the materials that make the object what it is.

5. Take another visual walk as before, but this time when you pass a particular building, stop and study it closely. Try to picture it in detail, as to how it is built and what it contains.

6. Look closely at any wall in the room you are now in. Notice everything about it, the objects that are fixed on it or standing against it. Study the form, size, and proportions of everything connected with the wall. Now shut your eyes and try to visualize the whole at once. If you can't see the wall clearly, imagine the various small parts of the wall in turn, and you

will see how much clearer these are.

7. Study a picture or painting that is visually pleasant. Then close your eyes and reproduce it in your imagination. Keep visualizing parts of the painting or picture, disposing of first one and then another minor figure or object, until your concentration is totally on the central point of the image. Hold that concentrated image for a moment, then begin to visually expand the picture until you once again see it as a whole.

8. Study a small object such as a statuette from a little distance such as the center of the room. After examining it, close your eyes and imagine it clearly from the position you have studied it. Next, imagine how it looks from the back by imagining you are now studying it from the opposite side, without actually moving there. After you have been able to visualize both front and back in your mind, try to imagine them both at once, as if you are looking at the objects from both sides at once. This exercise teaches us to remember that usually we have a very limited point of view in most things.

9. Look closely at a simple object such as a flower or a box of matches. Look into its interior, then close your eyes and imagine it. Imagine that your consciousness is at the center of the article and that you are looking at it from within. Next, expand your consciousness gradually until you are no longer a point in the middle of the object, but have become a large ball with the object in the middle of yourself.

10. Select an object you have already used in your exercises in concentration, such as the painting. Now instead of visualizing it first in parts, call it to your

mind complete. Make the whole picture spring up before your mental vision, in idea or in form.

Wood also offers some physical exercises which can aid us in concentrating better:

Try sitting completely still for five or ten minutes, without supporting the back above the waist, with your eyes closed. Your body probably will try to rebel in many ways, but do your best to remain as still as possible.

Another exercise in stillness is to try to stand erect and perfectly still for five minutes, preferably in front of a long mirror and with a clock or watch in sight. Your eyes can blink, but don't allow your body to sway, and pay no attention to any slight tingling sensations. Keep your mind focused on the different parts of the body, seeing that they are all still. Practice this for five minutes each day to improve your ability to achieve calm and stillness.

Supplement the stillness exercises with the practice of relaxation, which can help relieve bodily tensions. To exercise relaxation, take up a book in your right hand and hold it firmly in front of your chest. Raise your left elbow almost as high as your shoulder, and let the left hand and wrist rest on the book so the left forearm is roughly horizontal. Imagine slowly withdrawing the energy of your left arm until you feel there is no life in it, that it is very relaxed. Then suddenly drop the book. If your left arm falls as though lifeless, you have achieved relaxation. This exercise works even better if you have someone else hold the book for you and then remove it without warning you.

You can relax your whole body by lying flat on your back on the floor (not on a bed or couch) and trying to sink into it, as if it were soft. Another whole-body exercise is to stretch the body, then the neck, then letting it go loose and relaxing the body part by part, beginning at the feet and going up to the head.

In order to relax the eyes, which tire more than we realize from constant demands upon them every day, imagine the color black. It is good to relax by visualizing black this way before going to sleep.

Stretching and bending are other good exercises to aid in concentration. Stand with your heels together, raise your hands over your head, bend forward to touch your toes without bending the knees. Return to the upright position and reach as high as possible, standing on your toes.

Stand with your hands at your sides, palms inward, and lean slowly to one side until the hand on that side sinks below your knee, while your other hand is curled up under the armpit. Slowly swing back to the other side, stretching your body all the time.

Perform both exercises with concentrated thought for about one minute each. Then stand, raise one foot from the floor by bending the knee, then lower it and raise the other, and run for one minute, without moving along.

Yogis recommend somewhat complicated breathing exercises such as breathing in at one nostril and out at the other. Regular breathing with the full use of the lungs, a useful exercise during study or concentration, can be achieved more easily:

Draw your breath in slowly and evenly through

both nostrils while mentally counting to eight, or for five seconds. Breathe out slowly and evenly, again counting to eight. Repeat this eight times. Don't hold the breath in the throat muscles, but hold the chest muscles out and the diaphragm down.

Next, fill you lungs with air as before and then, holding your breath as before, press the breath down as low as you can in your body by sinking the diaphragm. Next press the air up into your chest, without raising or lowering your shoulders, so your abdomen goes in. Press the air up and down this way, slowly and deliberately, five or six times. Slowly and gently, then breathe out.

A third exercise is to inhale the breath as before, press it down as low as you can, and draw in more air, so both upper and lower parts of the lungs are filled tightly. Then suck in and swallow more air through the mouth until you feel slight muscular discomfort. Release the air slowly, from the chest first.

These breathing exercises, says Wood, will help make the body "bright and cheerful, and counteract the natural suspension of breath outside the body which often occurs during strong concentration of mind, as distinguished from the suspension of breath inside the body which accompanies physical effort."

Now don't laugh, but you might be able to improve your powers of concentration greatly if you learn to be a good juggler.

"There is a pattern to juggling five balls," says Mike Vondrushka, head of the Illinois Juggling Institute, "which takes total concentration because it's going so fast, you don't have time to think where your hands are supposed to be. You're totally immersed in what you're doing. You have to take in the whole picture.

"Juggling is a good educational tool. It builds confidence, improves concentration, and it's safer than skateboarding!"

Vondrushka and other jugglers around the country are spreading the gospel of their sport by conducting two-to-four-hour sessions in juggling for younger elementary school children and up to three-day sessions for junior and senior high school students.

"Juggling is a present-moment activity," says Dave Finnigan, head of the Juggling Institute in Seattle, Washington, who also holds a Ph.D. in psychology. "You can't worry about the past or dwell on the future. You're so busy working on three, four, five, six, seven objects in the air, you're totally wrapped up in that activity. The only reason a juggler ever drops anything is if he loses concentration.

"Juggling assists you in maintaining concentration. The longer you juggle, the more you concentrate. Juggling is an excellent activity to aid in concentration because it's a 'stepwise progression' of learning and dexterity. You start out by throwing and catching one club and build up to five or more. And it's an active form of concentration rather than a passive form.

"I've taught over 100,000 youngsters how to juggle. Lots of them had fairly scattered or diffuse educational backgrounds, many of them slow learners who had trouble concentrating on their studies. But after they became good jugglers, they found that their schoolwork improved. Juggling skills helped them to do other things better.

What happens in juggling is, you use both sides of your body equally, so there is a process called 'lateralization.' It is an important skill in the educational process. In lateralization you want to be able to scan, and switch from one side of the body to the other, so you are in effect bilateral and can use both sides of your body equally well.

"I've found that many children and even adults have trouble tracking, because they could only really concentrate on one side of their body or the other, and perhaps one eye was stronger than the other. In juggling, since you have to be able to use both sides of the body equally, you track, and as you track in juggling, so you track in reading. We've found that juggling has greatly improved reading skills in many children."

Finnigan says that juggling is now a required physical education class in many schools because of its educational benefits.

Many games also help develop our powers of concentration, such as checkers and chess, or Pick-Up Sticks, which was a popular parlor game some years ago. A new game involving skill, dexterity, and concentration for two or more players is called Ta-Ka-Radi Tiles. You stack the small oblong birchwood tiles one on top of the other in criss-cross patterns and try to take out the bottom ones without toppling the whole structure.

Space Invaders and Time Out are two new electronic games among many that are becoming very popular. Most people simply enjoy the excitement of playing the games, without realizing the educational benefits they are gaining from them through improved concentration.

One of the newest mind-developing games is Rubik's Cube, a favorite among both jugglers and mathematicians. Each of the cube's six faces is composed of nine smaller cubes, all connected to an internal core. Players rotate the cubes in various directions, attempting to put the cubes together so all the colors match. It takes a tremendous amount of concentration to remember where everything was, so you can put it back together again accurately. National and international competitions are now being held among Rubik's Cube players.

In starting to conclude this essay on concentration, it is appropriate to suggest again that the varied techniques and exercises for concentration offered by various men and women in this book can help us to live fuller, richer, and more productive lives. By concentrating on priorities, we can whittle down a mountain of tasks into a manageable few and attend to them one at a time until we have handled them all. We must learn to set "first" things first, and attend to them before we take on "second" and "third" things, in an order of priorities we set for ourselves.

Decide in what order you are going to concentrate on tasks or problems and then attack them, one by one. When practicing concentration exercises repeat the practices, and be regular in practicing. Try your own variations on techniques and exercises offered here.

Some techniques for concentration can be applied to many varied situations. My most consistently helpful "trick" to relax and get into a more positive, happier frame of mind is to combine deep breathing with mental images either of someone or some place I love. The place might be the wilderness canoe country of northern Minnesota and Canada, a five-million-acre paradise of natural beauty and undisturbed tranquility. When I am not fortunate enough to take a vacation that far from home, I find substitutes nearby. A few blocks from my home is a pond at whose edge I sit under two weeping willows to watch the ducks paddle by, to hear the sound of water lapping against some rocks, blocking out other sounds and creating a pastoral setting that allows me to pretend I am up in the wilderness canoe country.

In such a setting, I can forget the noises and other distractions which troubled me at home or work and find a mental state which allows me to concentrate, either on some leisure or the reading or writing I've brought along.

When you have mastered some techniques of concentration, when you have learned to bring all your mind and faculties to bear without distraction on the problem or subject at hand, you will find a twofold reward: Both the number of things you are able to accomplish, and the pleasure of accomplishing them will be immensely increased.

They say you can forget about a sore thumb if you get a worse pain somewhere else in your body, such as a sore toe. I had a sore back and leg while writing an historical novel set during the War of 1812 on the frontier. The pain was so intense I had trouble sleeping at night, yet when I was at my typewriter working on *Daughter of Winter*, I didn't feel any pain anywhere.

I wasn't even "at home" or on this planet. I was with the pioneers and Indians in 1812.

Any activity that totally absorbs us can help us forget about aches, pains, bills, and all other worries, if we truly concentrate on what we are doing.

Many people now are discovering that they can forget pain, even from broken bones or cancer, if they open themselves to hypnosis. Hypnotists claim they can help people stop smoking, lose weight, rid themselves of phobias, tensions, and other blocks to good mental and physical health.

Jim Stewart, for many years host of the television series "Passage to Adventure," has in recent years retired from that occupation to become a professional hypnotist from his home in Highland Park, a Chicago suburb. Asked about the powers of concentration a hypnotist must achieve in his work, Stewart presented ideas which seem appropriate to share in bringing this essay on the power of concentration to a close.

"In any meditation, spiritual or secular," says Stewart, "the concept of meditation is being in the *present*; being *here, now*.

"There is the story of the student who asked the wise old monk, 'What is the secret of happiness?,' and the monk tugged at his beard and replied, 'The secret of happiness—or enlightenment—is *attention*. When we eat, we must just *eat*. When we walk, we must just *walk*. In other words, whatever you're doing, pay attention to it.'

"These are ways of holding the conscious mind in the present," says Stewart. "It helps us from digging up the past, which can introduce our minds to anxieties which create fears. If we hold our minds in the present moment, it is impossible to create fear. We only create fear when we make a judgment about what will or might happen. We have to go into the past, to create fear. There is absolutely nothing to be afraid of, but a part of our mind may tell us to be afraid.

"We must gain control of our minds and concentrate on the fact—the truth—that *we* are creating our world. We are literally creating it with our mind.

"We don't have the foggiest idea of what the mind is, or who we are. All the greatest thinkers in the world, past or present, have or had—all any of us have—are theories. That's all anything is, a theory. Not a physicist in the world can tell us *what* light is. All that is known is how to create it.

"We all have to learn and explore and find our own truth for ourselves. And so many millions of people today are trying to do this. But the strange thing is, we are using the *mind* to find out *what the mind is*. It's like using your right hand to try to *hold* your right hand! But some drive in our subconscious keeps pushing us toward a better understanding, of ourselves and our world.

"The more we learn how to concentrate and put our skills of concentration to work for us, the more we will be able to draw upon the vast resources of our subconscious mind to help guide us in finding the answers we are seeking toward fulfillment.

"It is fascinating—and very hopeful to me—that today there are an estimated 35 to 40 million Americans actively involved in biofeedback, extra-sensory perception, self-hypnosis, and other forms of psychotechnology or studies of human consciousness. They are all asking themselves the crucial questions—'Who *am* I?', 'Is this *it*?', 'Is this all there is to life?'

Whatever the quests, we all have the answers, in our minds. More and more people are turning inward to their minds for the solutions to their problems, and it is my belief that they will find them there.

"For many of us, this journey is entirely new, perhaps often uncomfortable, even dangerous territory, and I am reminded of what Dorothy said to her dog Toto when they first landed in Oz: 'Toto, I don't think we're in Kansas anymore!'"

If we master our powers of concentration, they can take us anywhere we want to go. They can help us find solutions to questions or problems that beset us. They can help us get our work done more efficiently and with less effort and frustration. They can take us to heights of creativity and success we never dreamed possible, to find a new peace, harmony, and power within us.